THE
First Time
MANAGER

THE *First Time* MANAGER

M J MORRIS

KOGAN
PAGE

To Charles and Hilda Morris

First published in Great Britain in 1988 by
Kogan Page Limited, 120 Pentonville Road,
London N1 9JN

British Library Cataloguing in Publication Data
Morris, M.J. (Michael John)
    The first-time manager.
    1. Management
    I. Title
    658

ISBN 1-85091-482-6
ISBN 1-85091-483-4 Pbk

Printed and bound in Great Britain by
Biddles Ltd, Guildford

Contents

Table of Figures

What This Book Is For

This book is written for the person who is in exactly the position that I found myself in 20 years ago. Up to now, he or she has been employed to do a job with responsibility for just his or her own work. Now he or she has been promoted and is responsible for other people's work.

The new job may include the word 'manager' in its title or it may not. It may be called 'Foreman', 'Sister', 'Head of Department', 'Sergeant', 'Senior Planning Officer', 'Supervisor', 'Second Lieutenant' or any of a hundred other titles. What the jobs all have in common is that the people doing them stand or fall by the work of those who report to them.

The shift from the one type of job to the other involves profound changes to the skills that the individual needs to master. This book tries to do two things:

- to tell the new manager the things I wish someone had told me 20 years ago, which I had to learn, on occasion painfully,
- to take the new manager on a tour of the organisation to show the main work and concerns of the managers who work in the different departments.

My aim is to save new managers from repeating every one of my many and expensive mistakes, and to give them an idea of what is going on behind all those doors in other departments.

I must thank June Lines of Kogan Page for offering me the chance to write this book which is on a subject very close to my heart; and my wife Carole and daughter Nell for all their help and understanding. A husband and father who writes a book during the processes of moving house and changing schools is at the very least a burden.

Finally, a note on gender. Growing numbers of capable women are moving into positions of responsibility for others. It is only reasonable that their half of the human race should do so, breaking the near-monopoly held for so long by men. It does present a problem for the author, whose instinct dictates that he refer to 'he or she' and 'his or her' throughout. It makes for tedious reading though, so I hope that ladies will accept that the use of the male gender is not due to blind prejudice, but to regard for the reader.

Michael Morris

Chapter 1
Your New Job and Why You Are There

Management: fact and fiction

To many people the world of management is an exciting one full of beautiful people, money and power. To Hollywood directors and the more romantic TV producers that may really seem to be true. The people who actually inhabit that world know it to be very different.

To its practitioners, management is concerned with getting practical results out of difficult situations. In return for success they are awarded certain privileges. In every case, the good manager is more alive to his responsibilities than to his perks. When two or more gather together, the talk is rarely of wine and fast cars – well, no more than is healthy, anyway – but more often about problems they face at work and how they might tackle them.

One way in which management differs from many other types of work is that managers are not paid for the hours they put in. Instead, they are paid to get results. Frequently the targets set are far too high and cannot reasonably be attained. Many a manager will attest that the word 'challenge', used so much in recruitment advertising, is no empty cliché. To keep their jobs and to realise their ambitions, they face and overcome really testing challenges every day of their working lives.

Those who are good at it are paid well. Ask them about the rewards of their job, and the money, if it is mentioned at all, will figure low on the list. Most of the time the main source of satisfaction is in a job well done, in the glow of knowing they have pulled off what most people would have thought impossible. Perhaps it is easy for the well-paid to be cavalier about money, some might say. But most managers are not rich and would be in real trouble financially if they lost their jobs. Despite that, they stubbornly insist on getting their biggest kicks from making things happen, not from being paid well. Even so, most will bargain strenuously for higher pay when the opportunity arises: they do have their practical side, too.

If that brief description seems less attractive than the screen versions, it is not the managers who should be blamed. On the whole they are a hard-working group who take their work seriously. They have difficult balances to strike and maintain in a number of areas of conflict. Without their efforts, in the absence of people prepared to take on responsibilities, organisations simply could not exist. Without organisations nothing would ever be done that required concerted action by a large number of people. Our existence would be played out under the primitive conditions of the pre-industrial world, with standards of living to match. Not that managers are solely responsible for all the benefits of industrialisation – or its drawbacks – but theirs is an essential role in economic development. Without a flourishing economy, health and welfare services cannot be afforded, nor can national defence. Most people would think it desirable that those things should be available, however much they might quarrel about the forms they take.

As a first-time manager it is quite right that you should take pride in your new appointment. It is also vitally important that you grasp immediately that the rewards – pleasant working conditions, higher pay, longer holidays, and perhaps other benefits – carry with them an expectation that you will strive to deserve them. In that management is about getting things done, it resembles most other jobs. The unique aspect of management is that it does not do the work itself, but relies on other people to do it. Indeed, it is about getting other people to achieve the results. The manager does not get his hands dirty, but that does not mean he is idle. The nature of his work is different. It requires him to stop doing what he did in his previous, non-management, job and to take on a new range of skills and activities, and to adopt a completely new outlook. That sounds like, and is, the most significant challenge facing the first-time manager in the early days and weeks of his new job.

A further popular illusion should be disposed of. Some people think that 'management' is just a bundle of techniques. All the aspiring manager needs to do is study from books and – hey presto! – he knows what he needs to know. Techniques there are, and rightly so because they serve practical uses. They are no more to the manager than the tools a mechanic carries. Each one is designed for a specific task, and none is much use in the hands of the uncomprehending.

There may have been a time when promotion to management brought with it a meal-ticket for life, and a licence to appear at ten every morning and leave the office at four in the afternoon; not to mention the two-hour lunch-break. If those days ever existed they are long gone. If any exceptions still remain, they are in organisations which are thus demonstrating their fundamental corruption, and are doomed to fail. Tragically, the people who 'work' in this way will be unemployable when their organisations do eventually collapse, so soft will they be.

Management is a demanding calling, with no place for hangers-on. It makes demands not only on technical skill but on character too. Managers have to have a degree of courage, and they have to demonstrate integrity, as we shall see. It presents an infinite variety of challenges, some of them daunting and all of them fascinating, but the rewards for success are great and varied.

Your new environment

Someone who takes up an appointment as a first-time manager has to grasp the basic message about the nature of the field he has moved into. Furthermore, he has to find his bearings in a new organisational environment. Above all, he must find out exactly why he was appointed and what is expected of him. This information will help him to define and understand the new demands placed upon him and the new imperatives he has to obey.

It is not easy to do all of this under the interested scrutiny of colleagues senior and junior, of peers and of rivals. What makes it really difficult is that everyone shows this interest in the first-time manager when he is nearly totally ignorant about his job and his place in the organisation. Under such circumstances it is not easy to cut a dash. Indeed, it would be foolish to try. One certain way to make your sponsors really worry about their decision to give you this job is to shoot from the hip. A readiness to state firm opinions on the basis of little information and less experience is evidence of fairly advanced stupidity. There is an old saying to the effect that it is better to keep quiet and be thought a fool than to speak and put the question beyond doubt.

There are many people who want the first-time manager to succeed in his job. First, and most obviously, there are those who recruited you and do not want to be proved wrong; your success will be their success. Then there are your subordinates. They will take pride in working for a good boss in a section which is generally recognised as successful. Few people get much of a kick from association with failure, chaos and defeat, though such ghouls do exist.

There are also your colleagues from other sections, the smooth running of which depends on your section's performance. They do not want to be on the receiving end of poor output from your department. Finally, there are the people of goodwill whom you meet at all levels of organisations. They like to see someone doing well, and were among the first to congratulate you on your new post. Despite all the stories of corporate politicking that you hear, these people are around in greater numbers than some folk think.

There will also be a majority who do not care very much one way or the other. Those who have heard of you regard your appointment as just another fact of life. From time to time you will have dealings with these people, and as your career progresses they will grow to represent a constituency of friends or enemies, depending on how you behave towards them. Courteous and open behaviour at all times is becoming, and you will rarely know when a piece of behaviour will be noticed to be set in your favour or against you. This factor operates on two principal levels. There is the humble security guard or cleaner whom you always greet, and who gets into conversation with the chief executive about who comes in early and works late, and mentions your name; then there is the beefing session about you behind your back, when somebody whom you scarcely know speaks up on your behalf. In organisations all sorts of grapevines exist which are hungry for news to transmit. They reach right through an organisation: what do you want them to say about you? The best answer is probably 'Nothing, but if it has to be something, then let it reflect well on me.' Even if you do not attract too many strong supporters you can avoid making too many enemies. Do not overlook the fact that there will be a tiny number of warped personalities who will work to undermine you. They could be contemporaries or above or below you. Those at the same or a lower level are possibly worried that you will thwart their ambitions. There could be other explanations from a very wide range of possibilities. Those at more senior levels may have some private vendetta against your boss and try to get at him through you. Again, nobody should jump to what seems like an obvious conclusion. Human beings are complex and can have all kinds of contradictory feelings about their fellows.

Bear in mind that the enemy does not always come with a scowl and a raised club. A certain degree of reserve and saying no more than is necessary should get you safely past the individual who seems just a bit too friendly. You may encounter unusual incidents which could be interpreted as attempts at sabotage. The only way to deal with them is to use common sense and reason. Do not get drawn into arguments. If that approach does not work, withdraw with dignity and speak to your boss to ask advice. Later, when you have learned more about the internal tensions and the motivations of colleagues, you will be better able to deal with such matters unaided. Always behave with courtesy and do not become heated, however strong the temptation. Never respond in kind to someone who has lost his self-control: all that ever does is give the other side real grounds for criticism.

So much for the defensive side, of trying to avoid making embarrassing mistakes early on. There is a strong positive side to it, too. At first, people will not judge you by how much or how little you know, but by two other factors: how you behave personally towards them and others, and how you go about tackling things. A real drive to understand what the organisation does, and how it does it, earns a lot of Brownie points. Going about your job with energy, fairness and personal pleasantness takes you even further. People love to answer questions about their work, and their answers form a great part of your education. They will know you are ignorant and will be happy to help. They are flattered by your interest. So teach yourself and form relationships with colleagues at the same time, a game where everyone wins.

Up to now, virtually no mention has been made of the techniques of management. That is intentional, for the primary task in the first-time manager's early days is to show himself to the other, earlier inhabitants of this bit of jungle, so as to allow them to decide whether or not he is a threat, harmless, or a potential ally. That imagery is not entirely fanciful, since at an early stage of a relationship the most primitive instincts are in play. Those tribes of our ancestors who survived the early threats to their existence were the ones who made the right decisions about which interlopers to kill and which to admit to the cave. Because they are our ancestors, deep down we possess the same basic idea, that newcomers could be a deadly threat and must be treated with suspicion until they are known not to be hostile. Everyone knows how this works nowadays. A glance across a room may yield enough information to allow us to decide that we dislike somebody. Then we are introduced, and a few minutes' conversation shows that we have made an absorbing new acquaintance. We have witnessed the falling of the defences erected by primitive instincts for survival. These defences cannot be battered down: indeed, attempts to do so can result in reinforcing them. Only the owner of those defences can lower them, and then only at the rate that instinct will allow.

These ideas may seem strange to some first-time managers. Surely, there's a job to be got on with? And shouldn't everyone be judged on the basis of performance, and that alone?

Certainly, there is a job to be done, and urgently. But you would like to do it effectively and for some considerable time. It would be a pity to make much of that time more difficult than it need be. One way to do so is to ignore basic facts of human nature. An investment of a few hours in making people feel that you are a sympathetic and pleasant new colleague should pay off handsomely. Also, it may be true that the formal system says that every one is judged on the same impersonal basis. In that case, your performance should be all the more recognised, as your care with people will make you more effective in your job. Look at it the other way. In every organisation there is someone whose performance is always poor, yet who leads a charmed life because people like him. It should be nobody's ambition to emulate him, but everyone can learn from the way in which he insulates himself from the consequences of his results. Good relations with those around you can influence the way your performance is perceived, and hence judged.

Doing the job

When it comes to the technical side of the job, there ought to be fewer imponderables. If your boss has any wits at all he will make it quite clear what is expected of you and when, and will also define the minimum performance acceptable. The extent of your authority and the resources for which you are responsible will be named too. If, for some reason, this information is not available, you must request, demand and, if necessary, insist that you are given the answers in writing. Your boss will also arrange for your induction into the department's systems, and make himself available to answer your questions. He wants you to succeed – never forget that.

It may be that your activity is in a field in which success is difficult to measure. In that case, some numerical indicator could be devised which would reflect some approximation to the unmeasurable performance. An example of a field which abounds in such problems is that of advertising. Every advertiser wants to know how well his ads sell the goods, but there simply is no way of tying orders received from the trade to ads placed (there is an obvious exception where goods are sold direct to the customer from an order form on the ad itself). Instead of trying to accomplish the impossible, he falls back on measures which ought to have some relevance. The two commonest are the number of times people should have seen the ad, and their comprehension and opinion of it. By determining that people understand and approve of the ad's message, and ascertaining that they see it pretty often, he hopes that this means that the ad is doing its job of selling. Nobody really knows, though, yet advertising agencies and marketing managers sweat blood to raise those ratings to the highest levels they can.

There may be a temptation to flee from the very idea of targets. They do have great advantages to the manager, in that they state quite unequivocally what he is expected to achieve; there can be no disagreement or misunderstanding. The poor wretch with no measurable target may, for a time, think that he is on a rest-cure, but eventually someone descends from on high to demand why things are going so badly. All he can do in response is to squeak: 'Compared to what?'

One manager who had no targets for his unit asked what they were, but got no answer. He thought that this meant he should invent his own, which he did, and quite sensible he thought they were. One day his boss visited him to say that he was sacked. When, not unnaturally, he asked why, he was told: 'Things just haven't worked out.' That was as close to an explanation as he ever got.

So, if at this early stage the first-time manager encounters muddle and haze around the topic of targets and how achievement is measured, he would do well to keep his cv polished. The interviews he is called to he should attend, and the recruitment agencies he dealt with should be told he is still available. It would be wise not to tell the agency which found the present job, as they may stand to lose commission, and in any case may feel duty bound to tell the employer, their client. Organisations with muddled targeting and measurement systems and methods are doomed. Their fate will be to be taken over, to be run by a company doctor, or to fail altogether. Any of these implies cataclysmic change and consequent insecurity for the people on the receiving end. The question is rarely whether this will happen, but almost always when.

Morality

In dealing with colleagues at all levels, and especially with his subordinates, the manager must act with integrity. There will be temptations to economy with the truth, in order to have a quiet life. There are occasions when tact, compassion and common sense demand less than a full statement of one's beliefs, but self-preservation is rarely a sound reason. It is important, for trust is like life itself: you can lose it once and once only. The first time the manager is caught out trying to get away with something other than the truth is the last time he will ever be trusted. Trust is the basis of all your dealings with people. Once it has broken down, people suspect an unworthy motive behind everything you do and say, and will take nothing at face value. At that point the manager ceases to function properly.

There is more to integrity than just avoiding the telling of direct lies. It touches on every aspect of the manager's work. Not only does it forbid deliberate misrepresentation, it also means taking responsibility for events in his department. If one of the manager's people makes a mistake, he takes the rap in public. If one of his staff fails, it is his responsibility as the manager, and not the direct fault of that person: that is what he invites the world to believe and he acts accordingly. He shields and defends his people as much as he can, even if it would be easier and safer to let them take the blame. If his people make mistakes, it is the fault of his training and motivation, not their stupidity and carelessness.

Of course, nobody should attempt to defend the indefensible: people do have to take responsibility for their own actions, and accept punishment where due. But even the most flagrant abuse of the rules does not absolve the manager from his duty towards the miscreant. In such cases the organisation's disapproval will be registered publicly, and there may be nothing that can or should be done to save the individual from dismissal. However, the manager can speak in mitigation, can take a little time to speak to relatives, and can make sure that the person's good points are not overlooked by potential employers. The offender will accept his punishment as inevitable. He will also be frightened of the consequences of a blot on his record. The manager can help him to realise that this is not the end of the world, and that there is someone he can turn to for advice before the trouble starts again.

That is an extreme example. There are many more ways in which a manager can treat his people with decency and understanding while not infringing their privacy. His integrity tells him when he is in danger of interfering, rather than being available to help when needed. On occasion he will have to make the first move. A teenage typist weeping at her desk has to be approached rather than be left to ask for help. She can be offered the privacy of the manager's office while she regains her composure, and will value for ever the respect which that showed for her dignity.

Some first-time managers may feel that this is just a rehearsal of an obvious point about behaving with decency. For such people the reminder may be superfluous, at least in present circumstances. When the department is run off its feet and the telephone never stops ringing, it can be difficult for anyone to remember their people's right to respect. When the pressure is on, it is too easy to slip into treating your staff as an obstacle, rather than the means, to achieving your aims. From that position it is a short journey to regarding them as expendable cogs in the machine. If a manager ever reaches that point, his staff will detect it, however much he turns on the charm. That is the time when his licence to manage ought to be revoked.

It is not easy to decide what and how much your staff should be told. 'Economy with the truth' was mentioned earlier; the difficulty lies between, on the one hand, knowing that your staff have a right to know about the bad as well as the good news on issues which affect them, and on the other, that there are matters which are properly your concern alone. There is also confidential information which you may not disclose or even hint at. The manager who does let too much slip, in the hope of achieving a sort of camaraderie with his staff, runs great risks. His people see that he cannot be trusted with sensitive information and will be more reserved with him about the very things he needs most to hear about. The staff deserve to be told about how things are going: if things are bad, only a fool would pretend otherwise. The manager will talk about the situation frankly, within the limits of confidentiality imposed on him. He will also stress what is being done to remedy things, demonstrating that it is a rational response with a high chance of success. In this way he discharges his twin responsibilities to the staff and the organisation at large. As a result, the staff know that they may have to work harder and in different ways, in order to help the organisation or the department to turn the corner. They know why they have been asked, how important it is, and that it ought to succeed. In any organisation in trouble there coexist both worry and a willingness to help out. The manager encourages and uses the latter, and in doing so banishes the former. 'Things are going from bad to worse' is replaced by 'We are getting it sorted out.' There is a world of difference between the mental states which underlie each of those statements, and in the activities towards which each of them will direct energies. Worry is counter-productive; sorting out a problem is worthwhile and fulfilling.

Dealing with change

It is not unknown for a first-time manager to find himself pitchforked into a department with really major problems which he is expected to sort out. The staff know it; they know that changes must be made; they know what most of the desirable changes are, and they yearn to see them made. So many first-time managers disappoint them, for all the right motives. The manager may feel that they need a little stability among all the uncertainty, and holds back on necessary change. That attitude displays a becoming sensitivity but a wrong interpretation of the problem. Make the changes quickly, after taking a careful look, of course. Get the staff's ideas on what should be done, not forgetting to get the quiet ones to talk, check it with the boss and those colleagues who will be affected, and implement the changes. Your people expect you to manage, and to provide the conditions under which they can work properly and productively. Don't let them down or, if you must, explain why, show them that you have tried, and they will forgive you.

The first-time manager will find that his behaviour may have to be modified in other ways as well. If he has been 'one of the boys', he will have to withdraw gently to a more aloof position. If he has been inclined to act in a way which, coming from a manager, could offend or upset his people, he ought to think about making changes. An obvious example is bad language. It may be acceptable among former contemporaries, but it is definitely inappropriate in a manager. This has nothing to do with conformity to a boring stereotype, and everything to do with respect for others. If people are likely to be hurt by barrack-room terms the civilised person does not use them. The barbarian jeers at their prissiness and piles them on. There is a comic side to people's expectations of the sort of language managers should use. Many a strike by tough men in rough industries has been caused by a manager allegedly swearing at a man. Language that they use among themselves is, they feel, out of place coming from a non-member of their group who should know better.

The boss

Your boss also needs to be treated in a certain way. Not with servility: the cringing employee who calls everyone 'sir' or 'madam' clearly has so little self-respect that he can earn none. Given that your boss wants you to succeed, the only major area of possible dispute between you is any difference between his idea of what success comprises and yours. There might also be a subsidiary source of friction from the way in which you tackle the job, it is true.

One thing that the first-time manager realises early on is the truth in the perennial boss's moan: no subordinate can do his own job as well as the manager could do it for him. Some bosses stop at that point and never think further. Those with intelligence and a grasp of reality understand that, not only is that inevitable, but it may well be right and proper. The boss is usually older and more experienced, and ought therefore to be able to do most of his subordinate managers' jobs standing on his head. That is one reason why he is not employed at a lower level, where his ability would be under-used. Moreover, the superior has an advantage that the subordinate can never have: as the recipient of much of his junior's output he knows exactly what he wants and what is superfluous to his needs. Much as he will train his subordinates in producing what is required and not wasting time on extras, they will never achieve the degree of understanding which he can reach inside his own head.

If your boss shows signs of dissatisfaction with your work, the only course of action that makes sense is to show willing, and get him to explain what is wrong and what he really wants from you. This can be frustrating. One manager who did this got the reply: 'If you were a surfer, you would be forcing yourself through the waves instead of gliding along on top.' The imagery made sense to both sides, as the manager also felt that he had been working harder than should have been necessary. Nevertheless, he was getting results, so his boss seemed to be criticising style rather than output, although he could see a hint that output could be even higher if his style improved. As a guide to how he might do the job better, the remark was worse than useless.

That particular manager had previously reported to very gifted leaders and trainers. They all had in common the ability to analyse the way in which particular tasks were done, with constant reference back to the objective, which was the sole reason for doing it in the first place. With his later boss he found that he had to take the lead, and that when he did the response did not help much. Nothing daunted, he asked for five hours of his boss's time over the next fortnight, to allow for constructive criticism of the way he tackled a particularly difficult job that was coming up. He did the job just as he would have anyway, except that at each stage he told his boss what he had done and why, and how he planned to take things to the next stage. At the end of these confessions the boss was allowed to speak, to discuss the pros and cons of the way the work had been done. Both sides learned more about the way the other operated, and the junior manager found out a great deal that he had not known previously about the way in which his boss's mind worked. From then on, before making any move, he could ask himself how his boss would expect to see things done.

Some may see that example as a show of cowardice: the boss-monster should have been taken on and defeated, they believe. The sad fact is that, in real life, the boss wins such encounters 99 times out of a hundred. Moreover, it is just possible that the boss might be closer to the truth than his subordinate.

There is a general rule (apart from the general rule that all general rules are suspect), that governs the first-time manager's dealing with his boss, and with higher beings still. It is that most in-experienced managers give far too much detail in their reports to their seniors and in response to their questions. 'How are things?' is probably just a conversation-opener, or a request to be told if anything is off-target, and if it is, what is being done about it. Too many first-time managers will respond as if they have been asked the ancient Chinese civil service entry-examination question: 'State everything you know', and have taken it too literally. Just as the examiner was looking for the ability to isolate and address what is important and neglect the trivial, so the boss is looking for the ability to rise above everyday detail and provide an answer in terms that match his needs, not yours. The first-time manager who does not realise this is thought a fool or a smartypants.

Above all, be loyal to your boss. Whatever your private view, stick up for him when he is under criticism in the canteen at lunch-time. If his behaviour is so odious that you really cannot bear to defend him, at least do not join in. However tempting it may be, do not allow yourself to let off steam about him to colleagues. In the unfortunate event that it is clear to all that the man is an irredeem-able fool and a knave, do not try to deny the obvious but confine yourself to praising his good points (yes, we all have them).

The smae sort of loyalty is mandatory towards higher management and the organisation as a whole. However difficult to defend a particular decision or instruction may be, it is the manager's responsibility and duty to present it positively and constructively to his staff.

A famous American industrialist used to tell his managers not to give him any surprises. It is a good maxim for any first-time manager to observe in relation to his boss. If trouble looms, give him early warning. If stories about him are circulating, let him know. If he is away and someone senior looks in and asks questions, answer truthfully, but tell your boss all about it as soon as you can, and certainly before his boss has a chance to speak to him on his return. If there is anything about the man at all he will repay support like that, and your reputation for discretion and soundness will rise.

A final point on bosses is not to curry favour. Do not try to cultivate a social relationship unless you are encouraged to. Even then, do not presume on the relationship and expect favours. These are all further aspects of granting him due respect as a human being first, and as your supervising colleague second.

What do you want?

The spotlight now moves back from the boss to the first-time manager himself. You will have expectations of this job. It may be too soon after the appointment for you to envisage anything beyond learning the job and trying to survive in it. Or you may have been at it for some time and feel that you are getting on top. When that stage comes it is worth standing back and asking yourself some very fundamental questions about what it is all for. Every job can be seen as an educational opportunity. As such, it is a stepping-stone towards self-development. There will be aspects of it that fascinate you and those you dislike: one way of defining a good job is where the one does not outweigh the other. Fairly soon you ought to be able to decide whether this function is one in which you want to stay, and if not, whether you want to be in this field at all. A further dimension is that of whether the present organisation is right for you.

The whole point of this exercise is to make sure that what you do today and tomorrow is moving you in the direction you want to go. Chance can and will produce some lovely surprises, but it is a little uncertain as a basis for deciding what you want to do with the rest of your life. Conversely, people who make out that they have a career plan stretching from school to retirement, with defined moves every few years, are most kindly thought of as poseurs. We change, we learn more about ourselves, our environment changes and things happen to us that make more than medium-term plans useless.

The manager can never start too soon to think about what aspects of jobs he has held suit him, and which he dislikes. Over a period of time this process leads to a deepening understanding of what we really want to do, so that, before half your working life has passed, you know what you want to do with the other half. The knowledge may lead to a complete break with an earlier career, or it may mean exploring an interesting tributary to the main stream. Either way, it can make the difference between a working life of fulfilment and one in which one-third of your most productive years are spent in misery and strain.

Chapter 2
The First-Time Manager and Other People

Success with your people

Until now, your main responsibility has been for your own performance. Now that you are a manager you have suddenly acquired another responsibility. Not only do you have to perform well yourself, but you have to coax good performances out of the people who report to you. Indeed, your boss's view of how good you are at our job will be based largely on one factor: how well your people have performed.

This extension of responsibilities is always dramatic and, unfortunately, often traumatic as well. Handled badly, it can lead to a lot of misery for subordinates and a severe setback in the manager's career.

Just as any failure by the first-time manager to handle his people effectively reflects on him, so his failure reflects on his boss. If your boss does not realise this, you may need to bring it to his attention rather quickly and, needless to say, diplomatically.

Since you are not really keen to fail, but would prefer to succeed, what should you do? First, you should make sure that you never forget that your people's success is your success. There is only one way in which a manager can succeed, and that is through them. When a first-time manager comes to grief, it is usually because nobody told him that elementary truth. Having been promoted partly because he was good at what he did, he can easily assume that he now has to become twice as good at his old skill. Not so. Those first-time managers who have failed have usually worked incredibly hard. They failed because they spent precious time and effort on the wrong target: improving their old skills rather than developing new ones.

The good manager strives to understand what makes people in general tick, and looks in particular for what will help his people to fulfil their true potential. Inevitably, when you look at your team you will find people who are good at what they do and others who are not. Those in the latter category clearly need urgent attention. Firstly, you need to know why their work is below standard. The explanation usually falls under one of these headings:

- they lack technical skill,
- they do not understand what is expected,
- they have been told to do the wrong thing,
- they lack the desire to do well,
- their intellect is too low for the job.

That list is in a very rough order of probability, incidentally. Contrary to popular belief, there is a great deal that can be done about each item on that list. In some cases that may be obvious, but in others less so.

To deal first with the most intractable; the last item, where someone just seems to lack the mental equipment needed. It is, of course, perfectly possible that this is the case, but it is rarely so. The first trap to avoid is that of thinking that someone's inability to express themselves clearly is proof of stupidity. Skill with language is not given to all, and sometimes not to the brightest. Einstein did not speak at all until he was five, though he made up for it later. Just because somebody cannot talk fluently about a task does not mean that he lacks understanding of it. It can be equally dangerous to assume that the fluent talker has actually grasped what he speaks about. Moreover, the fluent talker may not be a doer.

Another factor to bear in mind is that there is a great deal of illiteracy around. People who have trouble with reading and writing develop all sorts of wily strategies for concealing their difficulty. Thus the person may not be stupid, just unable to cope with the level of literacy and numeracy involved. That sort of problem might be susceptible to a dose of training, but it will need to be done with tact and discretion.

It may be that the job is just not fair on the person. It might call for decisions about a number of unstructured situations which really ought to be dealt with at a higher level. Alternatively, it may be possible to create simple rules which are easy to follow, and remove the need to take decisions. An example is where customers' complaints are dealt with. Examination of their range and type shows that most of them fit into a number of clearly defined categories. If a list of categories is produced and guidance given on how to spot and deal with each, the scope for decision is virtually eliminated. The really difficult ones can, and ought to, be referred upwards. Thus the person's task is simplified, perhaps to the point at which they can handle it.

By such means managers help people to become more competent, less worried and hence happier. They also find that their section becomes acknowledged as a good place to work, with all the benefits that flow from high morale. The point of such helpful behaviour will not be lost on the colleagues of the person who was in trouble but is now on top of the job. Previously they will, by turns, have been exasperated by and sympathetic to the poor performer. At times they will have prayed for a replacement, at others, they will have wanted to help; indeed, they will almost certainly have tried. The appearance on the scene of a new manager warned them that trouble might be in store. The way you treat the weakest among them conveys strong messages about the sort of person you are and how you mean to behave. They were worrying about whether you were the devil incarnate or an understanding fellow-human with a job to do. The behaviour described will go a long way to earn respect, trust and cooperation.

Some approaches to the most difficult of the possible reasons for a person's poor performance having been considered, the other items from the list on page 26 can now be considered. If technical skills are lacking, the answer is probably to review the task to see if they really are needed, and if they are, to provide suitable training. Easily said, but sometimes difficult to accomplish. The help of a personnel and training specialist can be very useful in such situations.

Before any expert is brought in a little do-it-yourself analysis should be undertaken. A look at the task itself may throw up the most unexpected findings. It may turn out to be completely pointless, a result which is certainly not unknown. Often, when changes are made in organisations, odd jobs are overlooked which the change has made superfluous. Or the job may gradually have assumed an importance to the organisation which crept up on people because the movement was so slow. In that case you and your boss may decide that it ought to be upgraded, since the level at which it is being done now is just not adequate in view of its importance. In that case, training will come into it but not as an early response.

When redesign of a job is involved, do not be afraid to ask for views and ideas from specialists, colleagues, the boss and the job-holder, too. Far from losing points for appearing ignorant and indecisive, you will gain them for showing the wisdom to learn from others and to accumulate information before taking action.

Communication and motivation

The next issues on the list of underperformance factors were to do with unclear or inaccurate instructions. One of the greatest contributions that a management consultant makes when he reviews how a department does its work, is in his concentration on what the department *must* do. This means that he eliminates everything that does not have to be done. Usually he unearths activities which were once very necessary, but have become obsolete. Others, he finds, have somehow grown in the absence of any conscious decision to create them. Often they were proper responses to temporary problems; but when the problem died down the solution did not. It is easy to laugh and maintain that it could not possibly happen in your organisation. It does, for it occurs in every organisation on earth. The clever ones are those who recognise this inevitability and keep themselves under constant review to check these wasteful practices before they really get a hold. There is no good reason to leave the skeletons in your cupboard for some beady-eyed consultant or internal auditor to discover and make his name at your expense.

The remaining item on the list of reasons for underperformance concerned a lack of motivation. So how do you get people to want to do well?

Because so much hangs on the answer, that is one of the most-researched areas of organisational life. Armies of sociologists and psychologists devote their life's work to its study. The consensus of informed opinion boils down to three guiding, and somewhat conflicting, rules:

Long term, nobody can be made to do things: they themselves must want to do them.
The art of motivating them is rather like selling them something. It involves finding out what they want in life, and showing them how helping the organisation will help them to get what they are after.

People are different.
Some need the stick, some the carrot; some work best with loose guidance, others feel unhappy away from their tramlines.

People are the same.
They want to do well, they respond to encouragement, they like to know where they stand.

Later we shall touch on the research which supports some of these assertions. For the time being it is enough to say that most people will recognise them as broadly true in their experience, and do not need earnest and serious studies to persuade them.

A moment's reflection shows that people go to work from a variety of motives. Most of us need a certain minimum of money and are prepared to put up with a degree of misery to earn it. Some will accept a great deal of misery in return for large quantities of extra cash over and above their basic needs. Yet there are poorly paid people who love their jobs so much that they almost have to be thrown out of the building at night. Behaviour as diverse as this can be explained in all sorts of ways, but the single fact on which all psychologists agree is that: *behaviour is caused, it does not 'just happen'.*

The causes may lie deep within the person, or may be more superficial. They may be the result of upbringing or of inheritance. Whatever it is, the cause is there somewhere at some level. Just because you cannot identify the cause you must not think that it does not exist. Clearly, there is little that you can do to change the psychological make-up of your people, and it would be an impertinence to try. What you can do is to try to motivate them.

At the heart of motivation lie the two ideas of the person and the task.

The person
Finding out what combination of satisfactions will keep this unique person working to the limit of his ability, and supplying them

The task
Finding out what tools, systems, environment and resources are important to getting this job done well, and supplying them as far as possible.

Once those two requirements are satisfied, the argument runs, the person will be perfectly motivated. Of course, a lot can go wrong to stop the ideal from being reached. For instance:

- wrong diagnosis of the person's needs,
- the possible supply of satisfactions exceeds the person's appetite,
- the full complement of possible satisfactions is not being delivered,
- the job has been poorly designed,

- inadequate resources are supplied,
- the person lacks technical ability.

Then again, two people doing the same job side by side could easily rate very differently the importance of having this job, or any job at all. One might like going to work, the other hate it. One might see it as a job for life, the other as a stepping-stone. One might not care about the money, the other be very concerned about it. Even the most perceptive manager could not understand all that there is to know about each of his people. What he does grasp is that they, their motivations and their behaviour all vary, and he will strive to understand as much about them as he can.

Trying to understand the individual is difficult enough; it becomes even harder when there are laid over it the demands made by the job itself. Taken together, these problems conspire to stack the odds against any manager succeeding. This illustrates what a remarkable challenge it is to become an effective manager. Few who take up that challenge are extraordinary human beings. Those who do so, and succeed in that calling, can make an exceptional contribution to the lives of the people under them and the success of the organisation which they serve. Widely diverse types though successful managers are, the single thing they have in common is the ability to get people going.

What the research tells managers about people

At this point the first-time manager might wish that there was some simple set of rules governing human behaviour. Help is nigh.

Four major researchers have given managers insights into what governs the behaviour of people at work. They are Abraham Maslow, Frederick Herzberg, Douglas MacGregor and Elton Mayo. Their books are available from any academic library, but here we provide a brief summary of the light that each shed on the field.

Abraham Maslow
Maslow described how people seek to satisfy first their most basic, animal-like needs which are essential to physical survival. Once those are satisfied they cease to be of interest, and attention moves progressively to higher-level needs. Thus a man who was given £20 when hungry and wet would choose to spend it on shelter, dry clothing and food, but not, for instance, on a book. Once his low-level needs were satisfied by dry clothing, shelter and food his

higher-level needs would seek satisfaction, and he might look around for a book to read, or turn on the radio for music, or visit friends for company.

The lesson which this carries for the manager is that people need reasonable pay and conditions, but when those lower-level requirements are met, they start to look for other satisfactions, such as civilised treatment, liking their colleagues, finding their work interesting and believing it to be useful. The manager who does not realise this may try to solve all his problems with people by raising pay, for example. All he is doing is supplying more of a response to a low-level need than is necessary, and neglecting the higher levels altogether. Nobody is likely to decline the extra pay, but their dissatisfactions will remain.

Frederick Herzberg

The thrust of Herzberg's work was in much the same direction as that of Maslow, but it did contribute important additional dimensions. His view was that, in the modern world, motivating factors fall into two camps. Some are positive: their presence has a real and sustained effect on performance. An example might be the appreciation which a manager shows for an exceptional level of performance. Others do not motivate positively, but are nonetheless crucial. These are the factors whose presence is taken for granted, but whose absence does demotivate. Examples of such factors are sufficient income, adequate equipment or civilised treatment (and many more). These Herzberg labelled 'hygiene factors'.

The message in this for the manager is that today there are certain standards which he is expected to observe as a matter of course. He will get no medals for doing so, but if he fails to provide, his staff will be discontented. Quite separate from these are the real motivators. They include recognition, opportunity, appreciation and the chance to put one's personal stamp on one's work.

Douglas MacGregor

MacGregor's best-known work was to develop two stereotypes of managers. One, who operates on MacGregor's 'Theory X', believes that people need to be driven and will backslide if given the slightest chance. The view is that people are wholly selfish and untrustworthy. The other managerial type operates on 'Theory Y', believing that people really want to do well, and that it is the manager's job to help, encourage and inspire them.

31

Many people recognise that there is truth in both of these generalisations, and settle for a mode of operation somewhere between the two, adjusted as the occasion demands for different situations and different people. Clearly, when the building is on fire there is no place for a consultative meeting which seeks views on what ought to be done: the manager slips into Theory X mode and orders everyone out.

Elton Mayo

Mayo is best known for the 'Hawthorne experiments', run at the Hawthorne plant of General Electric in the USA (which is not to be confused with Britain's GEC). This work provided insights into the subleties of motivations at work. Brutally paraphrased, it showed that staff take little notice of the company's efforts to motivate them, or of its demotivating behaviour. The greatest influence was the degree of effort which they saw going on around them. The conclusion was that people do not want to stand out as either good or poor performers. Thus, whatever management does or fails to do, people will set their own pace and stick to it.

One interesting finding of the Hawthorne exercise was that output rose considerably in those areas of the plant in which the researchers moved, but fell back when they passed on. The feeling was that this was due to the boost to morale caused by becoming the subject of interest.

If anyone finds this field of interest, all these people are worth reading in the original. They published extensively, and any academic library, or larger public library, will carry their work.

Management Styles and Fashions

A first-rate way of making a fool of oneself is to propose as new an approach tried and rejected by earlier generations. Thus, while the first-time manager needs to know something of the current thinking among specialists in the management of people, he can also profit from understanding the shifts in approach which have taken place over the years.

In broad terms, the twentieth century has seen two approaches to the management of people. The Victorian era gave rise to the first-ever formalised theories of management, the so-called 'Classical School'. Roughly since the Second World War, the 'Human

Relations School' has held sway. Their characteristics can be summarised by the following lists of propositions.

Classical School

- The organisation is like a machine, enabling the person at the top to pull a lever to make things happen at the bottom.
- There is a clear chain of command from top to bottom.
- People are told what to do and how to do it.
- Human feelings are irrelevant.

Human Relations School

- Behaviour is influenced by attitudes; attitudes are affected by how people are treated.
- Better treatment results in better performance.
- Threats are very poor motivators.
- People want to do well and appreciate efforts to enable them to do so.

Echoes will be detected in this of MacGregor's two theories. It is self-evident that most people need to use both the X and the Y theories, either in a moving combination all the time, or separately as dictated by events. In any case, quite apart from any conscious decisions about their behaviour, managers come pre-programmed with a set of beliefs and values which, to a large extent, determine the degree to which they are instinctively authoritarian or liberal. That is no reason for abandoning all attempts to consider one's behaviour, for nobody should assume that the way his instincts dictate he behaves is necessarily the way to get results.

Ways have been developed of identifying and reconciling these different strands in the make-up of the individual manager. They seek out the extent to which he is dedicated to getting the job done ('task orientation') as against having friendly relations with colleagues ('people orientation'). People rate a particular score depending on the answers they give to a large number of questions. The mix can change – indeed, it must – with the situation. Thus a really hard-driving infantry officer, faced in exercises by the need to take a particular enemy position, will score nine for task orientation and one for people orientation. At night he may change completely, to a rating of three-eight, perhaps, in observance of the old army motto that officers eat last.

What else makes your people work?

So far some of the most important factors bearing on people's attitudes to work have been discussed. There are further influential matters to consider, under the main headings of *ability* and *preparedness* to contribute.

Ability to contribute is affected by:
- personality
- skill
- health
- training
- knowledge
- organisational setting.

Preparedness to contribute is influenced by:
- confidence
- motivation
- perceptions of the task, the boss, the organisation, and probability of reward and punishment.

Each of these factors will be examined in turn. Skills, training and motivation have already been dealt with.

Personality

People can be unfitted for a particular job in many different ways. An obvious example of a personality misfit is of an introvert in a setting where dealing with people is important. Thus the personality of the person needs to be matched to the demands of the job. By the same token, an extrovert required to work alone with no human contact will probably fail to perform properly. The wise manager bears all this in mind when recruiting, reviewing, transferring and promoting.

Health

People in good physical and mental health, given the right sort of work setting, feel as if they can take on the world and win. When they are under the weather even minor things can get them down. Many first-time managers are fortunate in having no personal experience of how health worries can affect people. These worries can be real or imagined, and they can apply to the health of the worrier or to that of someone close to him. The range of people close to each member of your staff may be quite wide: spouse, children, parents and in-laws, grandchildren, brothers and sisters – who could add up to a dozen or more – quite apart from friends. Thus at any one time there is quite likely to be at least one problem affecting everyone.

A worried person will not perform well, and may even upset other members of the team. The manager should not be too hard on him: if it has never happened to him he should count himself lucky, for it certainly will one day.

Knowledge

People who know the most are not always the best performers. Indeed, in some settings, they can be paralysed by indecision arising from their knowledge of all the things that could go wrong. That is not to argue against knowledge, but to say that judgement is just as important. The person who knows a lot but lacks judgement cannot take sensible decisions. Equally, somebody whose judgement is sound, but who has little knowledge of a particular field, is in no position to take a decision. However, he usually can identify the information he will need to bring him to that position. In the real world, knowledge and thought usually lead to understanding, which is the parent of judgement. Thus knowledge and practice in a particular field do tend to raise a manager's performance.

A manager should encourage his people to extend their knowledge and their understanding of their own field and of the setting within which the organisation at large operates. Study introduces new information, new perspectives on things and new ways of dealing with issues. To anyone interested in advancing their career it is an excellent way of preparing for promotion.

Organisational setting

As far as most of the manager's people are concerned, most of the time, he fixes the setting within which they work. The manager is the organisation for all practical purposes. There are matters which impinge on people over which the manager has little control – whether they can be allocated a parking space, pension arrangements, and the canteen menus, for example. However, in many ways what his people do and how they do it are largely fixed by the manager. He may not be able to change much in their working lives, but as long as his people recognise that he is doing his best for them, they will work all the better. To be seen to be trying to get better equipment, support, furniture, wages and so on will cause people to warm to you. It is better to succeed than to fail, but failure can be forgiven if sincere efforts were visibly made. It is important that this is done in such a way as not to raise hopes unduly: that could only lead to demotivation when the inevitable failure comes. However, even under the most unpleasant conditions it is possible for the most junior manager to ameliorate the setting in which his people work. Even in the most unpromising situation, the sense that you are brothers and sisters in adversity can help people to pull together.

Perceptions

This word may seem a trifle precious, but it is used because it has a precise and useful meaning. Psychologists use it to denote the impressions that people gain of events and things. Some people even argue that there is no objective reality, and that perceptions are the whole of existence. They would say that, because your shoe was hidden under the chair, you cannot prove it was there. You saw it go under, and you fished it out afterwards, but while it was out of sight there is no proof that it existed. Only while you were perceiving it through sight or touch could it be proved to exist. Furthermore, what kind of proof of existence is your perception anyway? You may be imagining the shoe for some reason. That line of speculation may keep philosophers and psychologists in work, but it is of limited use to the practical manager. Its value lies in drawing his attention to the idea that his way of seeing things is not the only way. 'Facts', 'truth' and 'reality', even in relation to the same event, mean widely different things to different people. Those differences arise for all kinds of reasons: social, cultural, personality, life experience and upbringing are some. All these influence how we see the world. Thus you, your supervisors, colleagues and subordinates are all carrying around different mental models of what was said, agreed and done. Even if you were all to agree on exactly what did happen (which is unlikely), there will be disagreement over its value and importance, and over whether and how to react. In other words, you all formed different perceptions of the implications of the event.

This variety is not something to deplore, but it ought to be recognised and taken into account in dealings with other people. Confronted by these ideas people often fall back in horror, demanding to know how, if all this is true, anyone ever manages to deal with any other person. Practical experience shows that to be an extreme reaction. Most of the time we manage to rub along reasonably well with one another. The manager is concerned with leaving as little as possible to chance, and therefore allows for the fact that his understanding may not coincide with that of someone else. That brings us to the next topic of this chapter, communication.

Communication

So widespread has the recognition of the importance of communication become, that this topic is almost a cliché. It would be folly if that caused people to think of it as something that little can be done about, a fact of life like the weather. It is an important matter, and a lot can be done to deal with its problems. The manager who cannot communicate cannot manage, so it is a matter of vital interest to the first-time manager.

At work it is essential that we communicate effectively with one another. On the simplest level, you want your staff to do something, so you tell them: you communicate. They do it and report back: they communicate. As has been seen, the human apparatus for transmission and reception is rather good at overlaying messages with all sorts of unintended meanings. Receivers can hear things never said, transmitters can say things in a way they did not mean. Chaos looms.

Chaos can, at the very least, be postponed, and even banished altogether. The key is to recognise the pitfalls already described and to allow for them. This does not mean treating colleagues like ignoramuses, but simply recognising the fact that you are all human beings and accepting everything which that implies. The same approach applies whether you are dealing with seniors, subordinates or peers, to ensure that each side is carrying away the message in the form in which it was meant to be put across.

One manager well remembers his first junior management appointment, when his boss wanted the new additions to the lorry fleet to carry the latest brand identity. Believing that signwriting lacked impact, and besides was costly and reduced the resale value of the vehicle, the boss said that he wanted plastic lettering that 'stood out', and could be removed when the vehicle was sold. The first-time manager thought he meant that the vivid colours of flexible plastic sheet, cut to the shape of the brand name, would stand out visually far better than mere paint, and would come off easily at trade-in time. When the boss saw it he said, tight-lipped, that this was not at all the effect he wanted. Then he explained that he had meant the lettering to be cut from rigid plastic sheet and bolted to the vehicles' sides, using spacers to make the letters stand proud. Boss 7, First-time Manager 0.

That manager now realises that if he had understood and carried out the intended instructions, the method would probably have failed. Either the plastic would have shattered from the general bumpiness of the ride, or drivers would have scraped it off when manoeuvring into tight spaces. Or it could have come off in the lorry-wash, or been torn off by wind-pressure at high speeds. None of that consoles him, for he now realises two things: it is important to check both the instructions he thinks he is being given, and that the instructions he gives are fully understood.

At the heart of this issue is the question of whose job it is to make communications work: the transmitter or the receiver of the information or instruction. As a general rule, both carry that responsibility in equal measure, but since the manager carries the can if things go wrong, it is in his interest to make sure that they go right.

The obvious technique available to the manager is simple and easy to master. It comprises passing the message, and then getting the person you are dealing with to play back what it is you want them to do. Most people know the childhood whispering game, when a message is whispered from person to person around a ring. Misunderstandings change the message as it goes, with the result that what started as 'send reinforcements, we are going to advance' becomes transformed into 'send three-and-fourpence, we are going to a dance'. (Readers unfamiliar with pre-decimalisation currency will be fascinated to know that three shillings and fourpence is equivalent to seventeen pence.)

That easy technique soon becomes second nature, but it should be applied subtly. People asked to repeat what they have been told will react waspishly. A subordinate can, instead, be asked how they will tackle the task. It will soon become clear if they are talking about a different job from the one you asked them to do. When you ask your boss to do something, you can ask what problems he foresees or where that information or permission might come from. Again, the reply gives away any misunderstanding.

When taking instructions from the boss it is important to check your understanding of them. A playlet:

First-time manager: Just to make sure I've got that right, you want me to get three units of 8080A into your office by ten tomorrow morning. Right?
Boss: Yes. *Or:* No, three dozen. *Or:* No, I leave at ten and I want to check them first; make it nine o'clock. *Or:* No, 8088. *And so on.*

The scope for misunderstandings is great, and when they occur the damage can be enormous. To reduce the risk of an occurrence, the groundwork starts before transmission begins. Listening is probably the most crucial element. The manager, transmitting information and instructions, must listen to his staff. The staff, the receivers, must listen to him.

Listening

Listening requires concentration and sensitivity. It therefore rarely works well when the listener is:

* tired
* angry
* emotional
* worried
* preoccupied
* suspicious
* unwell
* dying to say something
* in any other way distracted.

To make the listening part of your communication work well, you therefore need to do rather a lot before even starting to think about transmitting. If by some fluke none of the more extreme distractions listed above does apply, your people will be busy and will therefore have a lot on their minds. You have to start by wrenching their thoughts away from their present focus before you begin. It may take a minute or two, or longer. However long it takes, the good communicator does not start to transmit until he has gained the attention of his audience.

Once they are paying attention, that attention has to be held. This involves constantly refocusing it. Teachers who spot attention wandering bring it back with a jolt by asking a question, a useful technique at times. It must be borne in mind that on the side of yourself and of your audience there are further human problems to contend with.

Some more communication problems

* people hear compliments better than criticism
* prejudices and values affect perceptions
* reticence
* thinking about what has been said blocks reception of what is being said

- there are feelings behind the words which the words alone can only hint at
- not everyone listens actively, following the basic rules of good listening.

The rules of good listening are very powerful. Properly followed, they help you to understand and know your colleagues better, and to increase their respect for you. Every single piece of effective listening that you undertake improves your performance as a manager.

The basic rules of good listening

- banish distractions, physical and mental
- relax, and turn off the mental jabbering of your thought processes
- get the others to relax
- work hard at listening; aim to grasp what is going on in speakers' minds: what did they mean by this, why did they not say that? – show that you are listening: maintain eye-contact and if you have to break off or make a note, explain why
- as each point is made, play it back to check you have understood and to assess how others react.

Inevitably things will be said with which you disagree. This is not the time to argue back, still less to impose your point of view. There will be plenty of time for that later if it becomes necessary. Listening is different and separate from persuasion, but you cannot move on to the persuasive phase without it. Unless you listen effectively, you:

- do not understand fully the points being made
- do not really know what your colleagues are after
- have no idea why that point is being made now, in this way and by this person
- cannot gauge the other's sincerity.

Persuasion

The whole point of communication is to get something desirable to happen or to avoid some undesirable outcome. In order to do this people's understanding of events and their perceptions sometimes have to be changed.

Sometimes just passing information is all that is needed. The recipient receives it, interprets it and acts on it as you would wish.

Alas, for much of the time it is less straightforward, and the point you wish to convey is not accepted.

The first thought should be to give due weight to the objection, for it might be right. Many a manager has been saved from folly by another person's viewpoint. Even so, there will occasionally be courses of action with which we privately disagree, but which we nevertheless have to implement. If a matter is in that category it is pointless to stimulate discussion. It has to be presented for what it is, a *fait accompli*. After that presentation it is the manager's duty to make sure that it is seen in the most favourable light, but his loyalty should not go so far as to forfeit his personal credibility in the defence of the plainly unacceptable. Staff must be told that it is necessary and why, but the manager must not dissociate himself from it for that would be disloyal. When the reaction comes, as it will, the manager will say that he understands the objections. Then, and only then, will he try to fix attention on the future and how the changed situation is to be dealt with. He will paint word-pictures of how things will be under the new arrangements, getting people thinking not of what has been lost but of making things work. The explicit statement that resistance is pointless should be avoided, for nothing is more likely to stir free-born people to rage, resistance and even sabotage.

What the manager wants to see is all that energy of protest being channelled into solving the problem, which in this case is making the adjustment to a possibly unpleasant new situation. It may mean more work or fewer resources, or a removal of functions, or new methods or a score of other perfectly understandable grounds for grievance. Whatever it is, a manager's people will respect him if he gives it to them straight, accepts their right to hold and express their views, and then gets them to work on adjusting to the new circumstances. The manager will then be fulfilling one of his highest functions, that of reconciling his staff's best interests with those of the firm.

That was an extreme example, and deliberately so. Mercifully, not all the situations in which persuasion plays a part are charged with so much explosive potential. How can persuasion be exercised in this context? It becomes easier the better you and your people know one another. The basic rules are:

- listen to the objections
- acknowledge them
- show the positive side of the proposals first
- recognise openly their less desirable side

41

- explain vividly and simply how the net result will be a gain for the organisation, the department and the individuals.

If they still will not accept, the manager is faced with a choice between three courses of action: to withdraw, to revise the proposals, or to impose them. Withdrawal may cast you as a soft touch or as a wise person, depending on how you do it. Revision, if it is possible, scores highest for wisdom. Imposition forfeits goodwill, but sometimes it has to be done.

If you have honestly considered the objections and still believe that the proposal is, on balance, right; if you are certain that revision would fatally undermine the proposals' thrust and effectiveness; and if you believe that the cost in goodwill is outweighed by the improvements, your duty dictates that you impose the proposals. One of the things you are paid for is your judgement. If unexpected trouble does result you will be able to say with a clear conscience that you did what you thought to be right, that you had considered the consequences, and that the gains appeared to outweigh the advantages. In most organisations it is recognised that managers will make mistakes, as part of the process of making things happen. The organisations to avoid are those which are so risk-averse that their managers never dare do anything, for fear of getting it wrong.

When a manager has to impose he must explain that he is doing it and why. He should then ask the staff for their support in putting into practice the proposals to which they object. That may call for some courage, but nobody admires a coward, and no one said management was going to be easy. Again, it shifts attention to the future and what you are all going to do, and away from the past and the battle you have just lost.

Written communication

Oral communication is both easier and more difficult than its written counterpart. It is more difficult because of problems of vocabulary, concentration and mishearing. It is easier because it is simple to check the real meaning behind the words. Written communication does convey an authority which can be entirely spurious: the fact that it is in print at all makes it impressive. That can make it seem like the last word on the subject, to be obeyed however much it contradicts common sense. Then there is the problem of expressing yourself comprehensibly. Some people, who speak quite normally, freeze when they have to write. Their brain switches into a different gear, and they use terms like 'with reference to' instead of the word 'about', and close their letters with 'Assuring you of our best attention at all times' which is the biggest waste of typing time ever invented. The professional communicators who give the best example are journalists, particularly those on the mass-circulation papers. They use simple language and short sentences. They use the active voice rather than the passive (eg, 'I want to review the budget because it is looking increasingly suspect', not 'the suspicion under which the budget is increasingly coming means that it ought to be reviewed'). The first tells everyone what is to be done, why and by whom. The second has to be read twice to work out what it means, and even then it omits mention of who is to do the review.

Along with the need for simple vocabulary and short sentences goes the need to break down indigestible lumps of information into manageable morsels. If it is unreasonable to expect people to manage the whole lump in one go, feed it to them a point at a time. Replacing long sentences with tabulated lists is particularly helpful.

One rule of communication is to tell people where you want to take them before you start out. Some go-ahead organisations develop styles and conventions for documents. In case yours is not one of those, here is a suggested layout for a presentation to your boss, requesting permission for something you want to do.

1. Recommendation
What I think we should do.

2. Objectives
What it is designed to achieve.

3. Method
How I plan to do it, when and where.

4. Background
The situation that has made action necessary.

5. Implications
Costs, both monetary and other.

6. Justification
Reason for doing this and doing it now, risks, and risks of doing nothing.

A presentation like this saves the boss's time. Often he will see the sense of the recommendation, and without reading the rest he can approve it. Where he has to read on, at least he can see what conclusion you are leading him towards, rather than being kept in suspense until the last page.

An important rule is to keep things short. One highly respected international firm used to have a rule that no recommendation to a manager should occupy more than one side of paper. A rigorous discipline, it was to say all that needed to be said within that format, but it did lead to some strange antics. Some people used over-sized paper, others typed their documents normally, but then sliced them up with a razor blade into thin strips, reduced the spaces between the lines and then photocopied them.

Despite that, the underlying idea seems sound: that any recommendation should be capable of explanation and justification in quite a brief document. Managers' time is too precious to be taken up in writing or reading documents that are over-long. However, experienced writers will attest to how much more difficult it is to write concisely rather than at great length.

So much for the boss; we shall now return to the people whom the manager is responsible for. Depending on all sorts of factors, like the nature of the task, physical location, and the organisation's culture, you may need to write more or less frequently to them. There are some pointers to observe.

Written Instructions
- write clearly, simply and concisely
- banish detail to appendices
- draft and redraft until your meaning is clear
- if possible, put the draft away for a day or two, then look at it as if you were a recipient
- check with staff and departments that might be affected
- re-read it for accuracy and as a true reflection of what you mean
- if it is really important, get your boss to check for confused meanings
- put it through any necessary clearance procedures
- publish.

Even then the job is not over. When your people have read and discussed the document, go through it with them to check their perceptions and answer any queries about operational problems.

Power, authority and responsibility

Power can be intoxicating; some psychologists maintain that the urge to gain it is the mainspring which drives us. You tell someone to do something and he does it. You ask for something and it appears. All this is heady stuff.

On your first day as a manager, you sit at your desk. People look expectantly at you, perhaps even anxiously. They all seem eager to please. You must not let this go to your head. If you do, it will show that your idea of your job is exactly upside-down.

One of the things you are paid for is responsibility. In order to help you to discharge your responsibilities you have been given authority, from which flows whatever power you have.

It is not really your power at all. Rather than belonging to you, it attaches to the job that you are temporarily occupying. In the fullness of time you ought to gain a further source of authority, resulting from the display of attractive personal qualities. Equally, a bully or a wimp will find that his authority is reduced by the unattractiveness of his behaviour.

Thus authority springs from two sources:

- your position
- your qualities and behaviour.

The first is automatically conferred by the organisation to enable you to get things done. The second is harder to get, for it depends on people's judgement of your qualities and behaviour. They are not obliged to approve of them. That type of authority is easy to lose, too, for one good show is not enough – you have to continue to exhibit qualities and behaviour of which they approve.

One mistake which is sometimes made is to grant someone responsibility without the authority to discharge it. If you are ever in that position, lose no time in bringing it to your boss's notice. It is a basic principle in the design of organisations that authority and responsibility should be equal. Your boss should therefore be very glad that you told him. If he seems not to be, write to him confirming the problem's existence and the lack of authority to deal with it, and repeat your request to put things right. That covers your back, for make no mistake, you will get the blame for your failure to cure the problem. Then start to look for a job straight away. It is a rotten organisation and an inadequate boss who will let you take the rap for things you cannot control.

Leadership

Leadership is a vital part of the manager's job. It has already been discussed in part under the heading of Communication (page 37), where mention was made of the idea of getting people to do things that they do not want to do.

That thought introduces the very essence of leadership. It is the manager's job to get things done, and that is what he is paid for. He can try bullying and misusing his authority if he wishes, but will usually find that it creates bigger problems than it solves. The victim may do as he is told, but seethes at the slight on his dignity. From then on he will be bent on revenge, and may well succeed. It is usually not worth taking the risk. There may be very rare occasions when the damage to the relationship is less important than that to the organisation, but situations deserving this approach must be carefully selected.

The main elements of leadership are:

- creating an atmosphere of high expectations
- establishing clear objectives and guidelines
- setting an example of effort and achievement
- helping people to reach their potential
- acknowledging effort and achievement
- protecting and defending your people
- representing your department and people effectively
- treating people with respect
- and, if you possibly can, making it all fun.

Let us look at these points one by one:

High expectations

It is up to you to set the atmosphere in which your people work. Expect only a little of them and some might exceed the norm but the majority will learn that there is little point in making an effort. The true leader gets them to adopt targets that they believe are beyond their reach, then helps them to achieve those goals. Their awe at their own performance is exceeded only by their wonder at their leader's miraculous powers.

Clear objectives and guidelines

People become confused and irritated if they are asked for one thing and then expected to deliver another. That annoyance quickly turns into criticism of the person who confused them in the first place. It is a particularly effective way of earning scorn rather than respect; and respect is at the heart of leadership.

Setting an example
The boss who asks his people to put in great effort, but himself spends working time on the golf course, soon finds that his exhortations are ignored. Likewise, coming in late, leaving early, taking long lunch-breaks, inexplicable absences during the day – none is setting the right example to his people. It is even worse if they are penalised for lateness but he gets away with it.

So when you are going out it makes sense to let your people know where and why. They do not have to know all the details, but they do need to know if they will be able to reach you in an emergency.

Helping people to reach their potential
Your people are all different. They are diverse in their backgrounds, ages, circumstances, education, training, experience, personalities, beliefs, intelligence, abilities, appearance and ambitions, as well as in other ways.

Probably the most significant item on that list is 'ambitions'. People can be bright but content with their lot, and such people have their place on every team. Others will care passionately about getting on. This presents you with a dilemma: if you help them you will lose them, but if you do not, they might stay around for only a little longer. What should you do?

For once the answer is simple. If you help them you will get:

- good and improving results while they are with you
- a reputation as a developer of people.

If you do not help, you will:

- lose them more quickly to someone who will give them a chance
- be recognised as selfish.

Anyone inclined to promote his self-interest should remember that the ambitious subordinate of today may be the boss in ten years' time.

So much for those who are ambitious. There is another type whom you need to look out for, and who probably needs more help than the ambitious person. That is the person who cannot do his present job properly. The simplistic answer is to fire him but you could move him on to some other work. If he is clearly grossly inadequate in his present role, and is completely incapable of improvement, move him on to something new. He knows that he is bad at the present job and will be relieved to move on to something more within his grasp. Of course, the sack might be rather less welcome.

You have to be very sure in your judgement before taking such drastic action. There is, if course, the effect on the individual to consider. Then there are the practicalities: replace someone, and the chances are that you will get a replacement who is much the same in many ways, but has other problems it will take you time to uncover. For a start, he will have to fit into the team; then he has to learn the basics of the job. It takes at least six months to see if you have made the right choice – what do you do if you got it wrong?

On balance, at first it is best to give people the benefit of the doubt. Try to identify the cause of the problem, and only when you are as sure as you can be, deal with it. Identification can take a long time and cannot be hurried. First, the person has to learn to trust you. His first reaction on being asked a lot of questions by a new boss could be defensive. He may think that you are gunning for him.

You have to make it clear from the outset that you believe that he is under-performing. That presents you with the two obvious choices, to dispose of his services or to give him a chance – and you have chosen the latter. This discussion is in private, and you will give no hints to others about why you are paying extra attention to this person. Your aim is to help him to pull out of his past pattern and into a new one of success. You believe that he is capable of it, but only if he himself really wants to. Is he prepared to make the effort? If so, you will help, but most of the effort must come from him. Agree a timetable and a definition of success. Set out the rules under which he should deal with you, and ask for any questions.

If your attempt to solve the problem in this way fails, you will know that you had exhausted every possible avenue. If it succeeds, your reward will be the knowledge that you have done your job by the organisation and the individual. That person was in trouble and is now more effective and self-confident. His loyalty to you will be great. Such things are rare, precious and not to be under-valued.

Acknowledging effort and achievement
People like to be thanked for what they have done. You would think that nobody needed telling that, but it is a sad fact that few managers remember this elementary piece of good manners. Some

would say that doing their job is what people get paid for, and that they should not expect to be thanked as well.

That is a curmudgeonly view. It slips into the idea of people as mechanisms: pour money in and get effort out. It is well known that pay is certainly not the only thing that people get from their work. In any case, how can a manager possibly know when his people have made a great effort? What may be easy to him is perhaps a great challenge to his subordinates. It is folly to risk disappointing someone who has tried really hard by not acknowledging it. What incentive do they have to keep up the extra effort?

The most desirable thing to reward is achievement, of course. Nevertheless, people can come last and still contribute a lot to the department's accomplishments. They should not be ignored just because they did not take first prize.

The rewards themselves do not have to be large or expensive. Just a 'thank you' is usually quite enough. A brief explanation of how the department and the organisation have benefited is even better. Best of all is public acknowledgement.

Protecting and defending your department and people
Every organisation goes through difficult periods and, from time to time, every department comes under fire. Your people will be watching your response.

If your reaction is to turn round and blame the people under you, it is unlikely to impress anybody: your boss, your staff or your other colleagues. Insist that your people are good – the best group in the organisation in many ways – but that circumstances have not made life easy for them. Things would have been much worse if a team of that quality had not been on the job.

This goes as much for your dealings with individuals in your department as for the group as a whole. There is nothing to stop you from tearing strips off your people in private, but to the outside world you defend them. Even where their actions have been indefensible you have something to say. In those circumstances you do not try to defend so much as to mitigate. People whose bosses support them, especially in times of trouble, will go a long way to support them in return.

Representing your department and people
Just as you defend when attacked, if others are making it difficult for your people to do their jobs you get things sorted out. You do not do this in a way which will look to your people like surrender.

Furthermore, if your people have any justified grievances, you try to get changes made. You may fail, but you are seen to be trying.

Getting and giving the credit to your people for their good work is also important. Where somebody does something especially good you make sure that it is known about elsewhere in the organisation, and beyond if appropriate. Helping your department to build its reputation as a unit is important, and so is helping individual members of your staff to build their personal reputations. If a presentation has to be made to senior management on a matter which one of your people has worked a lot on, why make the whole of the presentation yourself? You could, instead, make it clear at the outset that you take responsibility for the presentation, but since Jane and John did all the background work on the project, you feel that they can explain it best: over to them.

Respect
You have a sacred right to your point of view, and so do other people to theirs. Much of what has been said so far can be classified as courtesy or good manners, an acknowledgement that the other person has rights, too. Good manners can be completely superficial; respect goes much deeper. Where your behaviour towards others springs from a fundamental respect for their rights, you are unlikely to misuse your relationships.

Insincerity, on the other hand, is detectable. Some are quick to spot it, others give the benefit of the doubt for longer. Either way, when it is eventually detected, it destroys goodwill, loyalty and motivation faster than anything.

Making it all fun
People do best the things that they enjoy. Why should they not enjoy their work, getting pleasure from personal achievement and being part of a winning team, and taking satisfaction from practising and improving their skills? The organisation's eight hours a day does not have to be a mental version of toothache. It has little to do with the number of hours people work – indeed, some of the people who enjoy work most spend a lot of time at it. Stories abound of 'hot' departments which work until seven or later at night which, on fiirst acquaintance, sound like the salt-mines. A closer look shows that people from other departments are fighting to get transferred to them; far from the present inmates seeking an escape route, they fight hard to stay put.

Such an atmosphere usually starts with one person, the

departmental manager. He or she does not have to look like a film star, or resemble a hero or heroine in any other way. What they do have is the ability to make their work fun; their enthusiasm catches and spreads, and before long the whole department is in a state of excitement. Everyone gets satisfaction and fulfilment from doing their own bit well, plus an extra kick from seeing the whole team succeed. The people who can create this atmosphere are rare, and some are exceptional in other ways as well. But what they do to inspire their teams can be learned. This means that nobody need give up hope if they cannot do it naturally. They can learn the skills and put them into practice, and will surprise themselves at the results.

Team building

It is hardly original to remark that people come with all sorts of different personalities. Some are leaders, or at least have in their make-up slightly more than the average ration of bossiness and the urge to control others.

When teams are being put together, or when an existing team is being reviewed, the question of personalities must be considered. If you want firecracker performances, go for people with a dash of leadership qualities about them. They will be difficult to control and downright argumentative, but they will make things happen all right. On the other hand, there are many tasks where individual initiative is inappropriate. Nobody wants an accounts clerk to exercise creativity in the way that the accounts are made up: sticking to the rules and the routine is essential.

The worst situation to create is one in which a bright, energetic, ambitious and competent person is put under someone who is defensive, jealous, petty and incompetent. Therefore consider the questions of personality type from all angles. Get the mix right in your team and it ought to work beautifully; if it is wrong, there will be trouble.

Health

Managers have available all sorts of tools to help them to carry out their jobs. They take great care to select the right equipment and to maintain it properly. They usually neglect woefully the most important piece of equipment of all, their own minds and bodies.

Keeping yourself fit to work is clearly a fundamental prerequisite of work of any kind. The threats to a manager's health are specific, and spring from the nature of the work. The causes of poor health include:

- a sedentary job
- the pressure of events: always more to do than there is time for
- worry about things that have gone, or could go, wrong.

Your people may also be exposed to similar or different risks, depending on the nature of your department's work. These risks pose real threats to physical and mental well-being.

Watch your people, and look at yourself in the same way. Are they tired and irritable? Unstable? Losing concentration? Drowsy in the afternoon? Putting on or losing weight? Taking frequent sick-leave? Constantly catching cold? All of these can be symptoms of stress or stress-related malfunctions, or of the ways in which people sometimes try to deal with them, by using drink or drugs. Time off for alleged sickness is noticeably higher among people performing routine tasks. They can suffer stress from constant pressure to do this work more quickly, and boredom from its repetitiveness.

Difficulties at work need not spring from work-related problems. Trouble in a person's private life can affect work performance. This is not easy for the manager to deal with, but it is his responsibility to do so. While he cannot help directly with the problem of a delinquent son or a sick parent, he may be able to reorganise holiday schedules or working hours to help someone to cope. It may seem little enough to the manager but it can be a godsend to a person under pressure.

People can also be worried by imagining that their work performance is not up to scratch. They are often right, and when they are they know before the boss finds out. By far the best way of dealing with this is through the staff appraisal procedure (if there is none, go and work for a firm that has one). This is a system which requires managers to report in writing on the performance and progress of each subordinate. In a proper system, the manager discusses and explains his evaluation with the subordinate; if there is agreement – and there usually is – a course of action and a timetable are agreed for improvement.

In a system where that is done once or twice a year everybody knows where he stands. They know which are recognised as their strong points, and they know what they have to brush up on. It eliminates large areas that people could worry about fruitlessly if left to themselves. It also concentrates their efforts at self-improvement on the right targets, as well as showing that support is at hand. It is therefore both humane and efficient.

Management style

Management style is a term used to denote the way a manager goes about performing his leadership role.

Managers are individuals, with their own unique personalities, backgrounds and beliefs. Therefore there can be no one style of behaviour which all should observe, a kind of mould into which they should force themselves. If they were foolish enough to try, either their insincerity would show or the strain of prolonged, successful pretence would take its toll.

There is no contradiction between this statement and earlier assertions that certain types of behaviour are desirable. While certain approaches to the job are of proven effectiveness, the way that different people put them into effect can vary widely. For example, someone who smiles rarely need not be miserable, just undemonstrative. When he bestows praise for a job well done it may sound gruff when compared to the way in which a more outgoing person would do it. That is not the important issue at all. What really matters is that he remembers to do it. How he does it is, and must be, a reflection of his unique personality.

Thus leadership style is not something synthetic which is donned as you walk through the works entrance. It is the real you, tempered and improved by your knowledge of how to get the best out of people.

Your boss

Some people think that the only thing that they ever need to do is to please their boss. Such a generalisation can be misleading and dangerous. Misunderstood, it could lead to crawling. The sort of boss you are better off without may be impressed by such behaviour, but anyone worth working for will not be taken in.

There is a wider sense in which your job is to please your boss. It depends on his being impressed by good performance of tasks which are in the organisation's best interest. His management style ought quite quickly to tell you what sort of person he is. He may be weak or strong, loyal or treacherous, competent or not. Whatever he is, you need to find out very quickly indeed. If he is a stickler for detail you will have to make sure that your figures are correct to the required number of decimal places; if he prefers a broad-brush approach, you can round up or down the odd hundred or thousand without doing harm. Until you know how the world looks from out of his eyes, your strengths might go unrecognised and your weaknesses may be floodlit. Thus, in the early days of your appointment you will be learning not only the job itself but also your boss's attitudes and values. You will be learning about what it says on your job description, and also getting to know the person upon whom your immediate career prospects depend.

Whatever the perceptions of your boss may be elsewhere in the organisation, there will be criticism of him behind his back. A pleasant man may be criticised as weak, or a hypocrite; an effective go-getter as ruthless; or an older person as tired. Remember the earlier discussion of loyalty, and say only those things that support him and which you would be prepared to say to his face. Apart from the moral aspect, there is always someone who will remember your words and quote them, carelessly or maliciously, in the wrong place. If you don't say it, you can't be quoted.

As time goes by you will learn more about your boss. If he is not good at areas in which you have strengths, demonstrate those strengths and leave it to him to take the hint. Help is rarely refused, but direct offers of help can be misunderstood. Where your boss has strengths, learn from him. A good manager is a keen trainer, and a session with one will teach more of direct relevance to your job in an hour than most business schools can manage in a week.

Do your boss's career ambitions coincide with your own? If so, and you work well together by complementing one another's strengths, you could make a team that will go far. As you get to know him you can explore and discuss the plans and aspirations that you both have. Inevitably he is able to control what you know of his aims better than what he knows of yours. In the best partnerships, which can occur at unequal levels in an organisation, the people concerned know each other well, openly acknowledge their strengths and weaknesses, likes and dislikes.

Your boss will have worries too. There are pressures on him that, to you, seem awesome. (In a few years' time you will be raring to have a go at them yourself.) How he deals with them and how he appears to you are tests of just the same sort as how you appear to your staff. Indeed, you can apply all of the manager-development ideas in this book to your boss. If he scores well on 70 per cent you have a very good boss indeed.

The most difficult boss to deal with is the one who fears you. He feels unable to do his job, observes your competence, and jumps to the conclusion that you represent a threat. His worries may be completely groundless, based on little more than a tendency to see plots everywhere. On the other hand, he may have seen contemporaries leapfrogged by juniors and believe that he is the next for the chop. Whatever the reason, there is only one course of action open to you. It is to do your job conscientiously, taking care that you present yourself to your boss as a loyal supporter. Any dealings you may have which could appear ambiguous should be recorded in writing. Even your own private, dated note of a conversation could clarify misunderstandings later. If the man is set implacably against you, at least you will have some basis for defence and explanation of the actions which he criticises. If mistrust springs from nothing more substantial than caution, open and loyal behaviour should quickly overcome the problem.

There may be temptations to educate your boss. They will be particularly strong if you are formally trained in management and he is not. If you really are convinced about the need for and desirability of introducing new ideas, explain them in everyday language. Technical terms should not be used: they will look like an attempt to appear clever, and nobody loves a smart alec. Ideally, it will not look as if you got it out of a book, but as if you made it up for yourself: it is just an idea that you thought might make things easier. If you fail to convince him, do not persist. Unlikely though it may seem, he just might know best, and if he does not, no amount of preaching will change his mind. You will just have to let matters take their course, and try again later if the opportunity presents itself.

Do not shrink from contact with your boss's contemporaries in the organisation. At first they will judge you by him. If he is not much good you need to establish your own reputation, independent of the department's. If he is good, your job will be so much easier. So whenever you have contact with them let them see how organised, on the ball, thoughtful and knowledgeable you are about the organisation's operations. Needless to say, none of that should be done so as to create the impression that you are putting on a special display, for nothing would count more against you. One day you may find that they have taken over your department, or jobs may come up in other departments. Being known already will do you no harm at all.

Your boss's boss

Inevitably there will be times when you come into contact with this august being. He will be on the look-out for many things when he visits your department, one of them being talent. Like any astute person, he will be singularly unimpressed by any showing-off on your part. Just deal with his questions politely and positively. Remember that if he was born in the 1920s, 1930s or 1940s he was brought up in a very different world from today's. When he was at school, most teachers wore their academic gowns to work; Frank Sinatra was the latest, most corrupting pop-music influence; and one's boss was always addressed as 'sir'. He knows that the world has changed, in some ways for the better, but he will be reassured to find that there remain a few of the old standards. Rising from your chair when he enters the room and keeping your hands out of your pockets cost you little, and will be valued by him.

One thing that you do not have to do is to tell your boss's boss the whole truth about everything in the department. Try to keep to the positive things, and when asked about those negatives which are not your responsibility, try to refer the question elsewhere. If the negative is a matter under your control, answer truthfully about the problem and tell him what you are doing about it. It is important that you both support your boss and do not look shifty. This man is no fool, and can spot evasiveness and disloyalty at 50 paces.

As far as you can, try to talk to the big man only about those matters on which you have complete knowledge. Do not discuss anything beyond your competence; and explain why you are confining yourself in this way. He will respect you for it.

Organisational culture

This topic has nothing to do with a box at the opera, but a very great deal to do with how you behave, how you are treated and, in the end, whether or not you are happy in your work.

Every organisation has a 'culture', a tradition of what things are important and how things are done. For example, the popular view of the culture of the Civil Service is that individual initiative is to be avoided at all costs. Initiative can lead either to successes, which are not rewarded, or to errors, which are punished. Doing everything by the book at a careful pace avoids error. Whether it takes a long time or fails to please the customer is not considered, as long as the action (or inaction) can be defended.

That caricature may not be accurate, but it is firmly entrenched in the public's mind. It portrays one sort of culture which suits some people well, but destroys the minds of others. On another hand, there is the more flamboyant, results-oriented organisation, in which sales growth is the idol. There the sales department are top dogs, and everyone else is expected to service their requirements. In a further example, say, of a professional practice, the ethical standards laid down by the governing body of the profession set the tone of the whole organisation.

The culture manifests itself in every aspect of the life of the organisation. This includes the way in which its people are treated and the behaviour expected of its managers. Some organisations look to their managers to all but break the law; others will dismiss them for unethical, albeit legal, conduct. Organisations still exist which perpetuate Victorian class divisions in their culture. Their behaviour suggests that managers are so superior that their needs cannot be met by the canteens and lavatories allotted to ordinary folk. A manager should seek out such an organisation if the common people make him feel ill. Even then, he might ask how he, as a relatively lowly being in the hierarchy, will be treated in turn. Life can present unnecessary problems for the manager if his bosses really do believe that redecorating the directors' lift is more important than replacing his secretary's clapped-out typewriter and broken chair.

An organisation whose culture is out of step with the times is in danger. Where the discord is between its corporate values and those of the manager, it will be an unpleasant place to work.

Chapter 3
Can Your Organisation Survive?

Why should you care?

The longer you intend to stay with an organisation the more this question will matter to you. You will also care if you are trying to build an impressive-looking cv. It will do you no good to be associated with a collapsed organisation or one which got into a lot of well-publicised trouble.

Whether or not your organisation is likely to collapse is therefore an important question. The power to predict its failure may seem well beyond the first-time manager. However, the techniques used by experts in this field are available to anyone, and the main ones are described in this chapter. It is usually a lot easier to predict *whether* an organisation will fail than *when*. Indeed, many an unfit organisation chugs on for years despite all the warning signs. Nevertheless the first-time manager needs to recognise as soon as possible whether to pursue his career with the present organisation or to create an escape plan.

The question of fitness to survive is not entirely defensive, about whether or not to leave a ship that seems to be sinking. It can be used equally well to evaluate a potential employer.

While the private-sector firm is the type of organisation most likely to fail, bodies in the public sector do die as well. They can also have large areas of their activity closed down or hived off, leaving a much smaller core which offers fewer opportunities and less security for individual managers. The public-sector specialist sometimes has resaleable skills, but many jobs in that sector are unique to it. Someone whose job is to draft bills for Parliament cannot sell that skill to anyone but the government, for instance.

The event which best illustrates the vulnerability of the public sector is the 'quango hunt' of the early 1980s. (Quango is the acronym of Quasi-Autonomous Non-Governmental Organisation.) The government of the day decided that there were far too many of these bodies regulating aspects of life quite unnecessarily, and abolished hundreds. Against a sea-change of that magnitude there is little the individual can do. It is too glib to say that they should have listened to the rhetoric and seen the trouble coming, for much is said by politicians which, for one reason or another, does not get carried through into policy. It was simply not possible for people to make realistic escape plans and, even if they had, they would have moved themselves on to a labour market which was shrinking dramatically.

The quango hunt was followed by a review of training boards. That was in a different category of activity. They were not to be abolished wholesale, but only those doing an effective job were to be preserved. Some were recognised as doing valuable work and continued in existence. One of those which were not so lucky was abolished for apparently very good reason. The review body reported with relish that it was unable to say how many establishments there were in the industry in which it specialised. After 15 years of service to that industry the reviewers felt that it ought to have understood some basic facts about its market. Whatever the state of its knowledge, it was easily foreseeable that one day someone would ask that question. The board was fatally deficient in those antennae which ought to have told it about problems which had not yet arrived, but which were over the horizon, lying in wait. Its more alert staff doubtless spotted this deficiency beforehand, realised the implications and got out in time.

Public organisations can fail in a less comprehensive way as well. They might attract insufficient support in the form of resources to do the job that they were set up for. In those circumstances they will fail their customers, their masters and their staff. The staff will get the worst end of the deal, being simultaneously overworked, abused by the customers and criticised by their masters. Eventually someone decides that setting that body up was not such a good idea after all and either abolishes it or amalgamates it with another, to the detriment of the staff interest. Rarely does someone admit to underfunding and give it more money.

Organisations, society and the law

Organisations come into existence for a reason. Usually it is to accomplish goals which an individual alone could not reach. Those goals may be in the interest of society at large, or they may be designed precisely to attack them. Even criminal conspiracies are organisations, and obey the general laws governing them.

Whether set up to accomplish good or evil, all organisations are capable of behaving in a way that attracts disapproval. For that reason society puts curbs on them.

Most societies agree that there are some necessary functions which can be performed effectively only by the state. The obvious example is defence of the realm. It would be an unusual government which put that out to private contract. By contrast, there are societies that are organised so as to have the state undertake all kinds of jobs that most of us in the western democracies take for granted to be the province of the private sector.

All societies try to limit the excesses which the private sector can be tempted to perpetrate in the pursuit of profit. The attempt to set such controls at the right level is an important preoccupation of legislators. Thus there are powers available to local planning authorities to control development, at the same time as a requirement that decisions are neither unreasonable nor delayed.

In the private sector a firm may feel itself tempted to take profit-seeking too far. It could reduce its costs by cutting corners on safety, or by not heating work areas adequately, for example. Society believes those expedients to be undesirable, and forces all firms to observe minimum standards of performance in these and many other fields. Thus the ideal of complete *laissez-faire* towards business has not been followed by any government in the UK for several generations. Enterprise is to be encouraged, but has to be tempered by care and concern for customers, suppliers, employees and the natural environment.

There have been governments under which such restraints have been felt by some firms to be excessive. Internal trade in the domestic market may have been little affected, for everyone had to play to the same rules. The disadvantage was more keenly felt when competing with overseas firms, either when they were attacking our market at home, or when we were trying to export. Here the higher costs which British firms incurred by compliance with regulations put them at a competitive disadvantage. Even so, in competing with firms from the developed world the imbalance is not so great as when the rival comes from a developing country. In the mature economies there is a broad consensus about unacceptable behaviour by business, so that the compliance costs may not, in the longer run, be all that different. Indeed, some manufacturers from West Germany suffer much more stringent controls over pollution than do their British counterparts, but that may turn out to be a short-term effect.

The lower compliance costs in countries of the Third World and the subsidised prices of some communist countries pose greater problems to some parts of British industry. If there are few safety requirements and little welfare provision the people of a country may lead miserable and anxious lives, but their industry will be able to undercut that of other countries. The classic response of the developed world has always been to use technology to add a competitive edge. It may have been employed to reduce cost by automating production, or to raise performance by adding extra features. The new factor is effective global communications. Once it might have taken a firm in the Far East years to spot, understand and adopt a western development; now it takes months; soon it will be down to weeks or even days.

Together with this evening-up in the communication of technical and scientific advance, there has been development of the essential industrial infrastructure in the less developed world. A decade ago, only the developed countries could be relied on to produce the first-class engineering tools and dies without which few advanced products can be made. Today, Malaysia (to cite just one example) not only satisfies its local demand in this field, but also exports excellent tooling to Britain, cradle of the industrial revolution, and beats many British firms for quality, price and speed of delivery.

Thus the law is an important influence on organisations, but it is certainly not the only one to limit or extinguish potential growth. The first-time manager encounters it in a variety of fields:

Personnel	Selling and Buying
Recruitment	Contract law
Pay	Advertising
Discipline	Packaging

Manufacturing	Operations
Safety	Accounting
Pollution	Taxation
Noise	Company law
Location	Insurance
	Vehicles

That is far from a complete summary of the ways in which an organisation is controlled. It relates, furthermore, to only one type of law.

It is necessary to recognise that there are two main branches to the law, civil and statute. Statute law arises from Acts of Parliament, enhanced and extended by ministerial regulations, breach of which can lead to prosecution by the state.

Civil law comes from a very different source. Its roots lie back in the days when an aggrieved citizen could petition his chief or his sovereign to right a wrong, perhaps to stop his neighbour's pigs from wandering on to his land and grazing his pasture. The chief would hear both sides of the argument and make an order accordingly. Anyone who ignored that order did so at some peril. Later the travelling representatives of the Crown's judicial function, the judges, took on these tasks. Civil law is based very largely on precedent, recognising the wisdom of supporting past decisions and of trying to build a body of case law which grows more comprehensive and reliable with every decision.

Just as the rest of the village expected our ancestors to behave with due regard to their neighbours' interests, grazing their pigs only where they had the right to and so on, today a wider society demands that we all observe the same basic rule. Today organisations, too, are regulated, as well as individuals.

Most of the regulations which chafe industry must have been brought upon it by its own misbehaviour. Factories have long been forbidden to pour untreated waste into rivers, a measure which was passed because many did just that, poisoning fish and causing offensive smells. The same goes for smoking factory chimneys, and everyone accepts the desirability of that sort of control. Yet with the onset of grain-based monoculture in the 1970s, farmers were surprised to hear calls to ban the burning of surplus straw. They said that they had no other way of getting rid of it, and that alternatives would cause prices to rise. In short, they deployed the same range of arguments offered by polluters of an earlier generation, desperate to defend their right to spoil other people's enjoyment of life. After the initial outcry, the wiser heads in farming saw the threat of detailed legislation looming. They realised that this could be very undesirable, since a House of Commons comprising largely urban representatives might be capable of passing very tough laws indeed. They acted by creating a voluntary code of conduct which minimises the amount of burning and controls the danger to wildlife. They exhorted their farming colleagues to observe these voluntary limits in an attempt, so far successful, to avoid a comprehensive ban on the practice. The farming community well knows that it must not slip in observing these standards or it will risk the imposition of legislation.

If the manager pursues his own interest too hard and at the expense of others, therefore, he risks having matters taken out of his hands and seeing controls imposed on his behaviour. Obviously it is proper for a manager to seek profit as far as he can within the legal constraints. It is less easy to say what he should do about areas which the law does not control, but which are clearly beyond the pale in the view of most people.

It is difficult, if not impossible for the first-time manager to take responsibility for such a decision. Indeed, if he does so he is unlikely to find his superiors admiring his judgement: he should have recognised what was beyond his scope. His job is to bring the matter to the attention of his superiors, to spell out clearly the opportunities and potential difficulties he foresees. He should then do what he is told. If that does not square with his personal view of how the world should be run he can choose one of only two honourable courses of action: staying and fighting the decision, or leaving. Depending on the seriousness of the situation he may consider 'whistle blowing' (exposing the facts to the media and the regulatory bodies). That is an action which demands a high degree of conviction and no little courage. It poses difficult moral issues. For instance, to whom do you owe your ultimate responsibility – the firm which pays you or to society at large? Will your revelations harm the people who work for the firm more than they deserve? What right do you have to usurp the position of those who have legal and moral responsibility for the whole organisation? What makes your view of the hazard the right one?

On the other hand, the Nuremberg Trials, at which the Nazi chiefs were tried for war crimes, established that it is no defence to say that you were ordered to commit a particular offence against humanity. Sceptics have called the Nuremberg Trials view 'victors' justice'. These are not new problems, for even the ancient Greeks had a proverb: 'silence gives consent.'

Governments frame the laws which Parliament enacts. Governments are run by politicians. Thus politics are at the heart of regulation.

Many people affect to despise politicians, attacking them for lack of principle, fence-sitting and inability to give straight answers. But is it really their fault? Consider their position. They came into politics through convictions about how the world is, and should be, run. They depend for their position on satisfying their constituency party as well as a majority of their constituents. The politician is looked to both to lead and to reflect opinion – an impossible task.

One sage resolved the problem a mite cynically, but thoroughly realistically, by saying: 'There go the people; I must follow them for I am their leader.'

Organisations need to keep in touch with politicians if they are to understand them and, by doing so, influence the course and nature of any regulatory process. Politicians need to keep in touch with organisations in order to represent the full range of legitimate interest in the constituency. Inevitably, party attitudes will obtrude at some point in these dealings. Attitudes within parties can crucially affect the subject of this chapter, the organisation's ability to survive. An organisation in the public sector may find that one party is dedicated to building it up, and another to destroying it. Those in the private sector, in some special areas of business (armament manufacture, for example) will find that their very survival has become a political issue in recent years. They thought that they were simply engineers in a specialised field, but find that they are branded exemplars of the enterprise principle by one party and merchants of death by another. Little can be done to change such entrenched attitudes, but a lot can be done by senior managers to limit the potential damage to the organisation. This is gone into in Chapter 5.

The grip of the past

At various times in our history the past has seemed to many people much more attractive than the present. In some parts of our national life colourful rituals display our taste for pageantry. Sober-suited members of the Establishment who would never dream of wearing a loud tie dress up in gorgeous robes of red and gold, encrusted with gaudy jewels. They do not keep this odd behaviour to themselves, either. Their processions through the streets of London and in Parliament are often televised. Even more inexplicably they would be perplexed at the antics of primitive people who did much the same as part of their tribal proceedings.

As long as this is seen for what it is, a ritual marking the continuity of the constitution and the rule of law, it does no harm. It even does some good in the tourism field, for it attracts paying visitors to Britain. The potential for harm lies in the assumption which can creep up on individuals and entire nations, that it is entirely right to continue automatically to do what we used to do, and that it somehow becomes more right the longer we do it. It is so much simpler to follow precedent than to innovate, and anyway making changes always causes such a fuss. It is easier all round to keep things as they are.

Just as the old ways grip the form (though, one hopes, not the substance) of the way the country is run, there is a great temptation to steer organisations by the same lights. The temptation is not an idle fancy: there are titled people who find it worthwhile to advertise their availability to adorn boards of directors, with no other distinction than their title to commend them. This really does happen, and it is an extraordinary reflection on the staying power of the idea that the aristocracy is somehow better than the rest of their fellow citizens.

Many organisations have senior managers and directors with ambitions to earn gongs. Things are changing as the meritocracy rises, but the charm of a title is a long time dying. There are some encouraging signs. In parts of the City, once a haven for the denser variety of aristocrat, people who are actually good at what they do are being recruited in preference to the titled incompetent (which is not to say that all titled people are incompetent, of course).

People at the top of organisations face a remarkable challenge in trying to stay up to date. They are selected both by and for their experience, all of which was necessarily obtained in the past. They are expected to chart a way into a future in which the events of the past may be an unreliable guide.

The classic illustration of this problem is of the two giant American mail-order retailers, Montgomery Ward and Sears Roebuck. Following the First World War there was a slump and mass unemployment, as the heroes returned from the trenches to factories idle now that there was no demand for war materials. The directors of Montgomery Ward determined to learn from that experience, and in 1946 deliberately kept their company from investing in expansion. They knew that many of the first casualties of a slump are those who invest heavily in expansion just beforehand. Sears Roebuck directors either did not know their history, or chose intentionally to ignore it. They spent heavily on expanding their company and the market. They were thus able to cash in on the post-war boom in the USA, leaving Montgomery Ward far behind, a position from which it has never recovered. With hindsight, Sears Roebuck's wisdom is clear. But hindsight was not available in 1946: what would you have done? The answer is not easy.

Every manager carries in his head a mental model of the organisation. The view of someone at the top will differ markedly from that of his juniors, a fact which he could learn by eavesdropping in any canteen.

Their views differ for all sorts of reasons. They come from different generations, they have different experiences of life (nobody born since 1942 has served compulsorily in the armed forces, for instance), and the direction taken by their education and training were almost certainly different. Even down at the level of goods and services which today we take for granted, there are markedly different experiences and expectations. Consider these dates for the mass-marketing of commonplace products:

1950s TV sets
1960s Foreign holidays
1970s Electronic calculators
1980s Home and personal computers.

This means that someone born in 1965 has never known a time when these items were not part of life. He or she may be in their first management job, reporting to someone born 30 years earlier, for whom none of these things existed until his adulthood. In his youth, the boss would have gone for entertainment to a dance-hall, or the cinema, or listened to the wireless. His transport would have been bicycles, buses and trains. He grew up in the anxiety and confusion of wartime. His schooling involved no artificial aids: major multiplication and division was carried out with the help of logarithms, and certainly not calculators, though he may have been introduced to the slide-rule in the sixth form. Holidays were at the seaside, usually in a boarding house. It was a different world and it made him a different person. People do adapt, of course, but they cannot alter what was irrevocably fixed in their early lives.

Built into each of us is a tendency to hold on, to a greater or lesser extent, to the past. Most of us do not like change very much, and that is a major handicap to adaptation to a changing world. Its evolutionary value is that we also do not rush to embrace the novel, which may turn out to be not only new but also dangerous. The risk to organisational life is that we hold on to the old ways for too long, delaying changes which may bring great benefits until we are forced to adopt them. Some managements are good at evolving, sensing changes in the environment and reacting appropriately to them. Others are certain that the present course is not only right, but will remain so for the foreseeable future. Too often they begin to consider the need for adaptation just as they step over the cliff. A purblind approach can and does cause organisations to fail.

An organisation which is so governed will change eventually. Regrettably the change is usually more costly the longer it is delayed.

Even more regrettably, the pain too frequently falls not on the architects of the problem, but on the employees and owners. When change does come to the rigid organisation it makes it snap catastrophically. Major closures and sackings take place, sometimes leading to the economic devastation of whole communities.

Survival of the fittest

Running through the imagery used to describe the successful organisation are vocabulary and concepts borrowed from biology. In nature, the successful organism is one which adapts to the environment in which it finds itself, acquires the resources it needs for survival, and establishes itself in sufficient numbers to ensure survival through even major catastrophes. If an organism is too cautious in expanding its population when conditions are favourable, it will be pushed out by more aggressive competitors for the same resources. If it is too greedy, it could strip its environment of resources and die out, or make too many enemies among competitors. Thus the successful organism occupies niches which it can dominate, but if it is to continue in existence it must take account of changes going on both within the niche and around it. In order to do so it needs three abilities, to:

- sense information
- interpret information
- create appropriate responses.

The parallels with the life of an organisation are obvious. To know what changes are taking place it must have the means to get information. Those changes may be taking place in its supplies of essential inputs – capital, raw materials, equipment and premises and people. Merely knowing that things have changed is not enough; there must be assessment, evaluation and interpretation to make sense of the situation. That must be followed by a decision whether or not to change, and if so, in what way. Making the change may be costly, but it is usually preferable to the alternative of increasing feebleness and eventual extinction. It should be emphasised that here we are dealing with the species as a whole, not with individuals. They will inevitably die, but the species lives on. It is the same with organisations: individuals come and go, but the existence of the organisation as a whole continues.

The rigid organisation, deaf to the increasingly urgent messages from its environment, runs down gradually until it fails, or falls to a predator. Its decline is usually in a series of steps, each larger than the last.

The adaptable organisation, on the other hand, recognises the danger of rigidity. Even if it is not proof against all that the environment can throw at it, its positive pursuit of appropriate change will mean that it is in better shape to endure.

The environment

The setting within which an organisation operates is complex. This applies with a vengeance to the large organisation, but even the smallest is linked to and affected by events over which it has no control and little or no prior knowledge. A plumber in a Scottish village is affected by the politics of southern Africa (where the copper in his pipes comes from), the threat of war in the Middle East (whose oil makes the plastics which he uses), and the state of trade with the USA (whose firms make many of his central heating controllers). Nearer to home, demand for his work is affected by the government's fiscal policies (which condition whether his customers feel well off and able to spend), the national economy (whether the banks and building societies have money to lend), not to mention the weather.

The environment of that one-man business is too complex for him to monitor directly. Thus, in order to stay in business he does two things:

- concentrates on just the key issues
- adopts surrogate measurements.

Instead of trying to keep up with all the matters which affect him, he picks the ones which really matter and concentrates on them. They are only few in number, so he does get some time in which to pursue his trade of plumbing. The key factors which he identifies are:

- enough work on hand, but nobody waiting too long
- prices not too high in relation to competitors
- prices high enough to cover costs and make the desired level of profit
- operating within his supply of working capital
- bank manager's forecast of the financial scene in three and six months' time.

That list is not too difficult to contend with. He can save a lot more time if he fixes a few of what might otherwise be uncontrollable variables. The cost of materials would be an example. He caters for variation by putting an expiry date on quotations, and by providing for prices to be raised to cover increases in materials costs.

A further way in which he has simplified the monitoring task is by using surrogate, rather than direct, measurements. Instead of trying to keep up with the financial wizards of Edinburgh and London, he lets his bank manager digest the signals and asks for his interpretation.

The robustness of an organisation relates to its stance towards its environment. Its culture, the quality of its managers, the strength of its finances, its technology, and where its raw materials come from are all factors.

To what extent can problems in these areas be predicted? It is possible to write a list of threats which could present themselves. It could include such issues as skills shortages, which are relatively likely to occur, as well as earthquakes, pestilence and flood. All are possible, but which are sufficiently probable to warrant inclusion?

Surprising though it may be, most commercial casualties seem to stem from major, long-term trends. In other words, a glance in the rear-view mirror would have yielded as much information as was needed to predict the future. When the Distillers group was taken over by Guinness its share of markets had been declining for years. The question was never whether it would be taken over, but when and by whom.

There is a minority of problems which can be just as devastating in their effects, but less easy to foresee. These are the shocks which are simple to list but unlikely to occur. When they do happen, it is therefore a considerable surprise. The obvious example is the sudden increases in oil prices in the early 1970s, when oil doubled in price, and then doubled again in the space of a few months. Its chief consequences were to plunge the world into a depression from which it has yet to recover fully, to create unprecedented concentrations of wealth in the Middle East, and to bring about enormous investments by oil-rich countries in the infrastructure of their own lands and the stock markets of the world. Anyone could have said that the oil producers might decide to raise prices, but nobody predicted when it would happen.

There are many forecasts around, all of which ought to be listened to but only some of which should be heeded. Those which worry us most are the most sensational. All are plausible, but the problem is often not when they will happen, but if. Examples abound of doomsday forecasts which have not come true – yet. One which did suggest the unthinkable was that which foretold the collapse of Rolls Royce. The forecast was ignored by most people, probably for two main reasons: it was incredible that Britain's premier engineering company could ever fail, and it was not put in such a way that it grabbed the attention. Perhaps if it had been promoted by someone more publicity-conscious than a British accountant, people might have listened.

The principle behind the forecast was financial. RR had decided to stop writing off research and development expenditure as it happened, reasoning that it was not an expense but an investment which would pay off in the future. This persuasive argument swayed the board of RR, but one academic saw through it. He realised that it would make RR think that it was richer than it really was, particularly in terms of cash. He even predicted when it ought to happen, 18 months in advance of the event.

There is only one piece of advice which can be given on how to tell the hucksters' forecasts from the real thing. It is to read them all, but to do so critically. Those which display a logic and consistency that cannot be faulted, while being in tune with the known facts of the situation, must be the most persuasive, however odd they may seem. At the same time, the view of the majority must not be automatically discounted. There is a way in which forecasts can be made not to come true, either because the warning was heeded and disaster averted, or the majority's stubborn insistence in marching to a different tune from that of the forecast overcomes the forecast's logic.

Takeovers and mergers

All organisations can be classified into two categories:

- potential takeover predator
- potential takeover victim.

It is possible for an organisation to fall into both categories simultaneously. A medium-sized organisation can be on the hunt for victims but at the same time be a larger body's next meal.

The brutal vocabulary of 'victims' and 'predators' is intentional. The word 'merger' is a polite evasion, for in every relationship of this sort there emerge a winner and a loser. It may take some time to become explicit, but the interests of one side do eventually prevail.

In assessing the fitness of a particular organisation to survive, it is particularly important to know whether it is more likely to be the drinker or the glass of water. Once upon a time the takeover targets were obvious. In the public sector they were very few, and in the private sector the bidders were easy to spot and their favourite targets simply identified. During the more turbulent times in which we live today, competition is so much more intense that there are more people on the look-out for acquisitions. At the same time, the environment has become so choppy that one organisation can be temporarily rising while another is falling, presenting an opportunity for one to bid for the other. Overlaid on that are the facts that an expansionary phase of the economy offers the finance to fund takeovers, and a recessionary phase makes all kinds of bargains available.

Then again, there are firms which are intentionally set up in order to be taken over. Their founders decide to create something which they can sell out after 10 or 20 years, and retire rich while still quite young. The purchaser might buy it with any number of ideas in mind. Most threatening to the manager is the situation in which his firm is bought in order to close down an inconvenient competitor. Next most threatening is where the assets are to be stripped and only a shell left in operation. Usually it is in the stripper's interest to leave at least a viable operation in existence so that he can earn money from operating it, or so that he has a credible business to sell on to another owner. In most cases, however, the buyer sees the purchase as enabling him to improve his grip on the market.

In looking at such a firm it is important to identify why a competitor might buy it. Non-competitors do not matter in this context, as their reasons for buying will be to get into the market: they will want to build up the victim rather than dismantle it. Competitors who mean to keep the firm running will buy in order to:

- increase market share by adding activities which they do not currently undertake
- get hold of technology
- increase the productivity of their sales force
- increase the productivity of their manufacturing assets.

Raising productivity means raising output per head, so they may well be looking for heads to chop off. Almost inevitably they will be in the victim firm. The part of that company which is to be closed will depend on the reason for the purchase. For example, if the victor wants to improve the productivity of his own factory he will close down the victim's and transfer production there. By such manoeuvres production could be rationalised, leaving selling un-touched, or the sales function be transferred to the new parent, leaving production as before. Sometimes both can be stripped out completely. The production and selling people of the victim company are at risk in either case. The administration, warehouse and distribution people are likely to lose out substantially in any event, for theirs are areas in which considerable savings can be made.

Should a manager therefore seek out an employer who appears to be takeover-proof? First, this question should be kept in perspective: traumatic though takeovers can be, many organisations are never affected. If it is a matter of personal concern – and it would be foolish to ignore it altogether – a significant division of one of the major takeover predators could be the safest place to be. Takeover-proof it may be, but the style of management exhibited by these firms does not suit everyone. Equally important, the sorts of opportunity offered need to be carefully assessed. Typically, such a firm is run very efficiently indeed. This means that it may be an excellent training-ground, but such firms do have the reputation of forcing the pace. If that excites and challenges you, put them on your list. If you doubt your toughness and resilience, think again; or have a go, but be prepared to move on if it does not suit.

By no means are all the results of takeovers bad. One manager in the sales force of a British firm of international repute tells an in-teresting tale. Under the original management he was unhappy: targets were high and rising all the time. As one who had risen from the ranks, his promotion was blocked because the firm made a point of holding back a number of key junior management jobs for recruits from the public schools. Not unnaturally, he was rather peeved by this.

That company was taken over recently by one of the specialists in takeovers, and many heads rolled at high level. The junior manager reports a far better atmosphere at his level. People are now judged by their results, not their school, and sales targets are much lower. Instead of chasing volume at any cost, the new owners encourage him to earn the maximum profit for the firm from the deals he does. Not only do the new owners talk better sense, they also listen.

Organisational analysis

Throughout this commentary runs the idea that some organisations are better-adapted to their job than others. So far we have not looked in detail at this rather generalised notion.

One of the most useful tools for assessing and comparing organisations is the SWOT analysis. SWOT is the acronym from Strengths, Weaknesses, Opportunities and Threats. The idea is to examine the firm's capabilities: what is it good at (strengths), and what is it bad at (weaknesses)? Then it is related to its environment: what opportunities are open to it and what threats are there to its well-being?

If this is done for one's own organisation and its competitors, a much clearer picture emerges of where they stand in relation to one another. It can greatly improve understanding of what is going on in a market, what could happen, and who the leading players would be. At the very least it offers the first-time manager some useful questions for the recruitment interview; at best it can point up major areas for attention.

The organisation which seeks to do the things essential for survival will be doing this for itself. It will recognise that the only permanent features of life are impermanence and uncertainty. Far from resisting them, it positively welcomes them because it knows that they will throw its less aware competitors off balance, while removing old problems and presenting new opportunities (and problems) to the alert.

Not every organisation is in that happy state. In order to be able to spot opportunities and to exploit them, and to identify problems and deal with them, it will be in a constant state of evolution. Since all the changes which the organisation makes to itself are responses to changes in its environment (or to its perception of it, which amounts to the same thing), the internal changes will follow the pattern described by those in the environment. Environmental changes are occurring all the time, on short, medium and long cycles. Short-run cycles are such things as advertising and promotional tactics, which can alter from month to month or from one season to another. Medium-run cycles concern matters on the time-scale of production technology, in which today's research breakthrough might translate into a new factory five years hence. The long-run changes are the really big ones, brought about by changing age-structures of the population, by changes to the distribution and amount of wealth, or by more fundamental technological innovation. Those examples are simply indicative, rather than complete lists in watertight compartments.

Readiness to adapt does not come about spontaneously, but needs to be caused by top management. The survivor organisation:

- has the will to succeed in the first place
- has a clear understanding that change is essential to progress
- has the ability to identify the right direction to travel
- provides the necessary resources
- creates the context for progress
- inspires its people
- achieves its goals
- defines new goals.

It also realises that energy is not enough; motive power has to be applied intelligently. It is therefore a thoughtful as well as a hard-driving organisation. It gives much consideration to the problem of information, the system for providing which can go awry in a number of ways.

Consider the process through which data must pass. (The distinction between data and information is important here. Data are individual items which, alone, give no real clues to a larger situation. Aggregated, they can give those clues, which is to say that they become information. An example is sales invoices: each one tells you something about an individual customer, but if you want to know how sales in total and by product and customer sector are doing, you have to perform some arithmetic and produce summarised totals. The invoices represent data, the summaries, information.)

First data are sensed; but the sensor may be faulty, or pointed away from the direction from which the true threat comes. Data are then processed into information; that processing necessarily reduces detail in order to allow the bigger picture to emerge. Part of what is lost could be an important pointer. Then the information is analysed and judgements are formed over its content and import, processes fraught with potential for misinterpretation. The next problem is that the solution designed may be incorrect; or even if a perfect plan emerges from all the problem-areas so far encountered, it may be executed badly.

Looked at in that light, it might seem like a miracle that anyone ever does anything even half right; or that it is no more than a happy accident when they do. Such fatalism may, on occasion, be realistic, but organisational life can hardly be conducted on the basis of crossed fingers and hope. Equally, nobody should ever fall prey to the idea that he is in charge of his own destiny. An awareness of all the things that could go wrong carries with it an important message: that constant attention to all aspects of its operations is essential to organisational survival.

The manager does not therefore try to watch everything all the time. He apportions his attention according to particular rules, which are discussed in the next chapter.

Chapter 4
The Principles of Management

The manager's role

A manager has a real job to do, a fact which is not always appreciated by those who report to him. It can look easy from the outside: a comfortable office, other people to do all the work, and a bit of glad-handing to do from time to time.

In fact, the manager's job is much more substantial than that. The organisation has its aims, and it is his job to achieve them by using the tools he is given. On occasion, the tools might not be adequate and he has to ask for more. However, the fact remains that the manager's job is to organise and control resources – equipment, materials, skills and money – to achieve the desired end.

In some organisations the manager seems to be expected to work out for himself what he should do. Where that happens he is the victim of bad management. It is unreasonable to demand that goals should be scored while the goalposts are hidden and the ball is invisible. In those circumstances it can be difficult even to tell which game is being played, football or hockey.

In any organisation in which reason and common sense play a part, efforts will be made to help managers to understand exactly what is required of them. Opinions differ over which is the best way of doing so, but there is universal agreement that it is difficult to achieve. That is not because there is stupidity on either side of the dialogue, but because of the eternal problems of communication between people.

Some organisations tell their managers at all levels what they are to do, expecting those instructions to be carried out with little or no discussion. Even where a different regime is supposed to operate throughout an organisation, there are managers who run their individual fiefdoms in that way. The trouble with this approach is that the better managers are not very good at implementing other people's ideas without question; being the people they are, they want to run things in their particular way.

Conversely, the sort of manager who prefers to cede individual responsibility to his seniors is not necessarily the kind of person who can play a full part in taking the organisation forward. Indeed, he is not so much a manager as an administrator, running other people's schemes as instructed. He is of a type found in every organisation, but most frequently in the public sector. One has to wonder where the next generation of imaginative senior management is to come from, if the pool available to draw from is full of grey administrators.

Naturally, there are occasions on which all managers must and will accept the discipline of working to goals which are not entirely their own. On the other hand, if the whole organisation is run completely on the principle that those at the top are omniscient, it will be severely and progressively impoverished. The middle-level people with a real contribution to make will leave in frustration. Those who remain will be quite incapable of succeeding the top management when it eventually retires or moves on. Thus one elementary principle of management is that nobody is ready for promotion until he has developed his successor.

Goals and targets

Clearly there has to be a degree of central direction in any organisation. It would be intolerable if everyone were to pursue personal interests and subjective ideas of where it should go. In many of the best-run organisations, which term includes departments within otherwise undistinguished bodies, the centre defines a target and states constraints. They might comprise a doubling of profits within the next five years (the target), to be achieved on 50 per cent more working capital (the constraint). When they have recovered from the shock of such a demanding requirement, individual managers can get down to interpretation into departmental targets.

The task is not then at an end. Ideas on how targets are to be achieved have to be developed into departmental plans. Let us say that the profits increase could be reached by a 70 per cent rise in sales (which would breach the working capital limitation) or by tripling prices (which would kill off too much market share). Thus each of these extreme routes is rejected, and a combination of extra volume, price increase, raw materials reduction, manufacturing efficiencies and financial policy changes is substituted. To get to that position there will be a great deal of negotiation and argument between departments, but once that point is reached each senior manager knows what he has to do to ensure that his department makes its contribution to the organisation reaching the overall goal.

Then the departmental managers can send the message down to their subordinates, defining what has been agreed as the department's contribution, and to what time-scale. It is then passed down from layer to layer of management, at each stage being broken down into progressively greater detail. Within departments there may be considerable modification of the overall rules, so that, for example, the lorry fleet may be allowed to think in terms of a steep increase in its costs and working capital requirement, provided that it is offset from elsewhere in the distribution budget (say, by closing one of the regional warehouses).

By such means every manager in the organisation can see what his personal contribution is to the grand plan. It is now each manager's job to work out in detail how he will bring it about. Figure 1 shows that this cannot be done in isolation: while some areas of responsibility are wholly under the control of a department, many concerns are common to more than one. Starting at the lowest level of the organisation, operating plans are formed. They feed up through the organisation like the sap moving up from the roots of a tree. At each higher point, the plans from the lower levels are pulled together, amended if necessary, and passed on upwards. The process of aggregation goes on until, at the top of the organisation, everything fuses into a single entity, the overall plan.

Bargaining, negotiation, pleading, manipulation, cajoling and bullying all come into play in this process. The first-time manager may simply be unable to see how he can possibly effect the economies or volumes required of him. Not merely challenged, he can be frightened by the scale of the demand. It is the responsibility of his superior manager to help him to raise his sights and concentrate not on how difficult it is, but on the way it could be pulled off.

Excellent performance is achieved by thousands of small acts like this throughout an organisation. Refusal to accept that yesterday's performance is good enough for today, pushing back the frontiers of what people see as possible – that is how organisations become great and maintain their momentum.

Figure 1 *How departmental interests overlap*

The overall aim

In order that all the subordinate plans come into being, the lodestone of the organisation's overall aim is needed. Its function is to unify and coordinate: by making the plans of everyone in the firm point in the same direction, it enables them all to pull together in the common cause.

This aim is often not easy to define. There was a short time, in the 1960s, when it became fashionable to define a firm's aims as 'making money'. Certainly that is preferable to making losses but, like pleasure, money-making usually results from the pursuit of some other goal.

Whatever the aim is, it must be within the organisation's powers to accomplish. More is needed than just a brilliant idea, or the ability to make a product or provide a service. Finance will almost certainly be required, and the skill to manipulate the various resources available. Moreover, the aim has to be consistent with managers' and shareholders' values. Usually, the attempt to define an aim results in the generation of a range of options. The test that should be applied to each option is the extent to which it is:

- desirable
- feasible
- acceptable.

The SWOT analysis (page 73) will have identified options which could be pursued. The management now applies this test to rank the various options in order of preference. Since judgement is at least as important here as measurable factors, there is great scope for an individual manager to make a personal contribution to the debate.

Major assumptions will have been made about the plans' acceptability to staff. Now comes the test of those assumptions, the point at which they are put across to people. Arriving at the definition of the overall aim and the resulting plan was a complex enough process; but it often proves simpler than making sure that the message is:

- received accurately
- understood
- accepted
- and, finally, implemented.

Too many well-formed plans have foundered in this process. They have been subject to one of the following problems:

- received inaccurately
- misunderstood
- rejected
- not implemented

and, as a result, have failed miserably.

Small wonder, then, that managers gave an enthusiastic welcome to a technique which promised to banish these problems for ever. It would make sure that managers at all levels knew exactly what they had to do. It spawned work for consultants like no other technique before it. It is called 'Management by Objectives', or MBO for short.

Management by objectives

This technique emerged after the Second World War, taking as its basis the idea that, running through the organisation there should be a clear chain of command, which should be exercised as the primary tool of top management.

Few would challenge the idea of people liking to know where they fit into the scheme of things, what they are responsible for, and to whom. MBO says that it is the job of the person at the top to set an overall objective, and to require his subordinates to show how they will contribute to its achievement. They, in turn, have their subordinates show what they will do to make sure that the objective is achieved, and so on down through the organisation.

In that way, the overall aim of the organisation is contributed to by every person in it. The top person ensures that:

- the issues affecting the achievement of the organisation's main aim are addressed by everyone
- the non-influential issues are ignored or deliberately neglected.

The mechanisms used to bring and keep the members of the organisation into line vary with the consultant offering the programme. Their common content is to require each job to be specified in detail, no bad thing in itself, and then to have each manager define and agree with his boss the key and lesser areas of his responsibilities bearing on success in his job. Then performance standards are agreed between subordinates and superiors. The main governing factors are also defined. Actual results are compared with the target for each area, usually monthly. Finally, any adjustment needed to performance is agreed for the following month, and so on.

In principle, MBO offers the top manager the power of far tighter control over what is done and to what standard: no wonder it appealed. Why, then, isn't everyone using it?

Nobody quarrels with the idea that people are paid to help their employer to reach the firm's goals. To the extent that MBO helps to bring that about, it can only be welcomed. Unfortunately, there are two key problem areas: paperwork and self-protection.

As has been said, different consultants sell different versions of the MBO package, but most seem to involve fearsome quantities of paper. Every month the middle manager has to report to his boss in writing about his performance against target. He also has to deal with similar reports from his subordinates, perhaps between five and ten of them. Meetings have to be held to discuss the reports. Some organisations have found that the real benefits of greater integration of the organisation's aims with the individual's actions are outweighed by the extra administrative load imposed.

Self-protection comes into the equation when people resist being too ambitious, for fear that they will create a problem for themselves in the form of ever-increasing targets. It can seem sensible to be careful, or even pessimistic, in the target you accept and the performance you deliver. Thus, the greater control which the top exercises under MBO becomes feared as an instrument of imposing ever-mounting demands. People protect themselves from the threat that they perceive, and performance gets worse instead of better; or nobody saddles himself with the target that he could achieve for fear of ratcheting-up expectations. A system designed to improve performance can therefore reduce it.

A further problem arises from the fact that MBO has to assume that a lot of the performance factors are fixed. The great interlocking pyramid of personal goals against which progress is measured is somewhat inflexible. Change the goals because the environment dictates it, and all the measurements have to start again against new goals. Couple that with the much leaner levels of staffing of management nowadays compared to those of some periods in the past, and there emerges a picture of too few people with too little time to erect paperwork mountains. Now that the computer is so common, and is easily able to calculate paperlessly the quantifiable factors of performance on which MBO lays such stress, MBO may be due for a comeback.

MBO has not been discredited as a management technique any more than the muzzle-loading rifle has become less able to kill at 20 paces. Its value is considerable, in that it showed not only the desirability, but above all, the practicality of integrating personal aims with those of the organisation at large. Perhaps its most abiding legacy is the emphasis which it placed on the central role of objectives. The truths which it popularised were by no means universally recognised before it came on the scene.

Thus, it has left an abiding message for those organisations which could make no use of MBO because of the mechanistic view of the organisation on which it is predicated. They may not be able to use an MBO package, but they need constantly to keep their objectives in view. An old people's home, a research laboratory and a design studio are examples of organisations which simply cannot be run satisfactorily as if they were machines. A large car assembly plant must be, and therefore could apply MBO with good results.

Management techniques: their place in your job

If you are paid to operate a particular technique, say a computerised PERT model (programme evaluation and review technique – a method of planning and controlling complex projects), used to control a large civil engineering scheme, that technique will play a big part in your working life. You are an exception among managers, since few of them find that any one technique, still less the whole range, is of use most of the time.

The whole point of the techniques, boiled down to its essence, is to help the manager to organise information so that the stage at which he grasps the point comes sooner, cheaper, more comprehensibly, or in any combination of these. At centre stage is not the technique, but the manager's understanding of the issue he is dealing with. Understanding is the end, the technique merely the means.

What goes for techniques also applies more or less to measurement. We measure where it aids understanding, and only where it is realistically possible. The idea of what can be measured may surprise many who left school with a perfectly respectable O level in maths. Statistical techniques exist which are rarely touched on at school, even today, but which greatly help the manager's understanding of his world. If you are lucky enough to work for an organisation which has its own statistician, see if you can get him interested in what your job entails. He might show you all sorts of short cuts and perfectly proper tricks with figures which will reduce the time you spend slaving over a calculator. At the same time, he should also be able to enhance the depth of your understanding of the quantifiable aspects of your job. One or two of the more elementary and universally useful methods are touched on later in this chapter.

Judgement, experience and training

Despite the emphasis on measurement which overlays so many texts on management, in the end the manager is there not to do sums but to exercise his judgement. That quality is exercised on information of both quantity and quality. Measurement greatly aids understanding, but it is the start of the process of management rather than its entirety.

The manager's judgement is honed by experience, a curious entity. Some people who claim 40 years' experience have, in reality, had one year's experience 40 times over. They have neither reflected on events nor developed understanding. True experience is gained not just via existence, but by observation, reflection and experimentation. In other words, a certain amount of effort is involved.

The part that experience plays can be seen when two managers, one experienced and one not, are confronted with an apparent emergency. The inexperienced one will probably dive immediately for the alarm button. His more experienced colleague will spend a little time pondering the evidence before acting. He may come to the same decision in the end, but does not lose an undue amount of time in doing so. The real value of his more considered approach lies in what goes on between his hearing of the problem and acting.

What the experienced person is doing is, basically, threefold:

- deciding to what extent he can trust the information,
- deciding whether or not he needs any further information, and getting it,
- reviewing the possible courses of action, and selecting one.

His experience helps him at all three stages. He has seen more examples of ambiguous information than his colleague, and he has given more thought to the way in which such information is generated and conducted. He has seen, or thought about, situations of this sort before, and can therefore more easily spot what conclusive information is missing. He is also able to create a richer list of options for action and is well placed to assess the likely outcome of each, and is thus armed to take a more informed decision.

The obvious course of action is not necessarily the best. Indeed, masterly inactivity might be best of all, in certain circumstances. An American statesman once advised his president: 'Don't just do something, stand there.' His experience told him that frenzied activity would achieve little in that case, and that an impassive pose would be the most impressive attitude to adopt.

Put to good use, experience does give a manager a head start. Having dealt with problem X a dozen times in his career, he hardly needs to think what to do when the thirteenth jumps over the parapet. The danger comes if he allows his preparedness to spill over into complacency. Seeing what looks like a problem X, the knee-jerk reaction responds automatically to what subsequently proves to be a problem Y, skilfully disguised.

At this point the less experienced manager could despair. What hope has he of gaining ten years' experience in anything less than a decade? Fortunately, there is quite a lot he can do. The answer lies in education.

Today's manager has laid before him without doubt the richest choice in management education since time began. If he can get to a major city there are various institutions vying for his custom on a wide variety of courses. Degrees and diplomas can be gained. Even out in the depths of the country learning is accessible. The choice of distance-learning programmes is ever widening and represents a greater range than the old-style correspondence courses could ever muster. The Open University, and more recently the Open College, are just two of the organisations which offer management programmes which can be followed at home and at the manager's own pace.

The whole point of formal study is to shorten the length of time it takes to learn. Much of what is taught the student could have worked out for himself; in that case, learning it on a course concertinas the time taken to acquire the knowledge. Other information which is gained on courses comes from far greater minds than the student's, and from disciplines which he has never encountered, so it can safely be assumed that he could never have learned it unaided. Study cannot and never will supersede experience entirely; it does complement it massively, and add greater depth to the conclusions that the manager draws from his day-to-day life.

Dealing with complexity

Many of the situations which a manager has to deal with are very complex. They often do not look like it on the surface, but digging for the underlying facts often reveals a complexity which was not at first suspected.

The human brain is a wonderful thing, but faced with a complex situation it can switch into panic mode. A better response is to stay rational and apply techniques for dealing with such situations.

Exactly what you do depends on the nature of the problem in question. In umbrella terms, you:

- classify

- assess for size and impact
- list probable outcomes
- list available responses
- assess likely consequences of each
- select action.

Take an apparently simple problem: a sudden fall in the orders coming into a children's shoe factory. The full explanation may lie in decisions taken in millions of homes up and down the country, about what shoes to buy and when. They all filter through into thousands of shops selling the merchandise; they in turn experience pressures. One may have the bank insisting that buying is reduced in order to lower the overdraft. Another may have stocked up with a competitor's brand. A third may have become fed up with slow delivery of orders and switched to another supplier. Multiplied out by dozens of possibilities across thousands of shops and millions of families, it adds up to an incomprehensibly complex picture. The manager should not lose his head, though. The complexity comes about because so far all he has dealt with are data; what he needs is information, the aggregation of data into meaningful, summary form. The main potential reasons for the problem appear on this list of six possibilities:

- competitor activity
- retailer liquidity
- retailer stocks – in total
          – of this brand
- consumer demand
- the firm's reputation and past service
- sales force abilities.

No manager in any market is incapable of listing the main possible reasons for a situation in just the same way. He will seek information which will test the situation under each heading, and reveal which is or are the most influential factor(s). He will not, however, take some of the evidence offered at its face value.

The sales manager will, most likely, excuse low sales by sickness in the sales force and the trade being full of unsold stock, despite which his team has battled on heroically and won the firm a higher share of the few orders around than it has any right to expect. Unfortunately, while evidence of that quality needs verification, decisions have to be taken fast about whether or not to put the factory on to short time. The cost attached to getting the decision wrong, either way, is high. What do you do?

Starting with the resource closest to hand, the sales manager, you ask him to find out quickly whether the cause is:

- competitors encroaching significantly on areas that we expected to protect
- high retail stocks of our brand because:
  − it is selling out of the shops too slowly,
  − Marks & Spencer have promoted children's shoes effectively,
  − the public is demanding competitors' brands more than ours,
- a general slowdown in trade through:
  − the usual seasonal demand coming in late,
  − changes to school holiday dates,
  − less consumer spending,
  − a credit squeeze,
- poor trade perceptions of our brand or our service,
- mass holiday, etc, absences in the sales force.

You must have answers to these questions, and within a day or two. Otherwise the unsold stock could clog up the warehouse and absorb all the firm's cash. What needs to be done is to reduce the effects of millions of individual buying decisions among consumers and retailers to just a few main questions. Each bears directly on your business. Thus an almost infinite variety of possible avenues of enquiry has been reduced to a dozen or so.

That is an example of relevant and appropriate reduction of variety, which has rendered complexity comprehensible. Had the list of questions been shorter, it might have risked missing some important point altogether. As it is, while there is a possibility that some important factor will be missed, the list above does cover most of the field. That list is therefore short enough to be manageable yet long enough to cater for the likely explanations. It avoids sophisticated economic analysis for two reasons: time was short, and it was in any case unnecessary. It was unnecessary because acceptable surrogate measures exist for those aspects of economic activity which affect purchasing decisions of children's footwear. The retailers' reports to the sales manager are close enough, and certainly adequate for these purposes.

Clearly, it is vital that you know the cause of the problem so as to assess its seriousness, decide if a response is called for, and choose the best response. If you thought that the problem was lack of consumer demand, you might have devised an advertising and promotion package. That would have incurred considerable cost, justified if it was the only way to keep the factory running, but unforgivable if the true reason had been the simultaneous absence of all the star salesmen. In the latter case, the sales managermight learn a few lessons about scheduling absences.

Statistics

Statistics is a branch of mathematics which managers find useful in:

- showing up patterns in past behaviour,
- showing correspondences between different factors,
- providing a springboard for forecasting.

All these could conceivably be accomplished without recourse to special techniques, so why should statistics be so useful?

As has been stated already, the manager's main contribution springs from his judgement. To be fully effective, it cannot operate solely on hunch and feel: facts have to come in somewhere. The most prevalent and useful facts available to a manager are numerical, and numbers are capable of being manipulated by the unwary into giving misleading guidance.

In the old days, before the early 1980s that is, most managers who wanted to use statistical methods had to learn a lot of formulae and how to apply them. The difficulty which most of us seem to have with maths at school rose again to haunt them. While it can be interesting and useful to learn the detail of the calculations, most managers today can avoid the number-crunching if they want to: the personal computer, or even the scientific calculator, will do the hard work for them.

Helpful though the computer is in doing the sums, it still needs to have the right numbers supplied to it, and the user needs to know which techniques to invoke in particular situations.

Statistics is a very broad subject, and most managers use only a very small part of its range. The areas of greatest use cover:

- probability
- distribution
- regression
- correlation.

To learn the ways in which these are calculated and the kinds of applications to which they are best put, the first-time manager can consult any textbook on statistical applications to management consult any textbook on statistical applications to management problems, using those headings to search each index. There now follows a brief sketch of each.

Probability

Probability is expressed as a decimal fraction: complete certainty is represented by a probability of 1; a 50–50 chance has a probability of 0.5.

Tossing a coin brings about two outcomes, heads or tails. Unless it has been tampered with, the chances of any one toss resulting in heads is 0.5.

Likewise, the chance of a normal, six-sided die falling on any one number – say, a four – are one in six, or about 0.167. The chances of any one throw resulting in one of any two numbers – say, a five or a six – are twice 0.167, that is 0.334. The chance of any of five numbers being thrown – say, any number between one and five – is five times 0.167, or 0.835. (It really should be 0.833, the slight inaccuracy arising from the fact that 0.167 is an approximation to three decimal places of 0.16 recurring. But in an example like this there is little reason to worry about tiny variations.)

To change from one example to another, 50 marbles will be used, 20 white and 30 black. All go into a bag, and one is drawn out. The chances of it being white are calculated at 0.4, thus:

Probability of white

$$= \frac{20}{20 + 30}$$

$$= \frac{20}{50}$$

$$= 0.4$$

This also tells us that the probability of drawing black would have been 0.6: it had to be one or the other, so that there was a probability of black or white of 1.0. Subtract 0.4 from 1.0 and the probability of black emerges.

Suppose that the ball which came out was, against the probability, white. If that ball is kept out and a second ball of unknown colour withdrawn, it will not carry the same probabilities. This is because the total number of balls in the bag and their colour-combination are now different. The probability of white is now:

$$= \frac{19}{19 + 30}$$

$$= \frac{19}{49}$$

$$= 0.39$$

Furthermore, the probability of drawing a second white after the first can be calculated by multiplying the two sums together:

$$\frac{20}{20 + 30} \times \frac{19}{19 + 30}$$

$$= 0.4 \times 0.39$$

$$= 0.156$$

That shows the chance of drawing two whites in a row as 0.156, or about one in seven. As is easily seen, probability is not a guarantee of behaviour, merely an indicator of what is likely to happen. In practical terms it shows that, over the long run, a pattern similar to that indicated by the probability figure is likely to emerge. Toss a coin five times, and it might come up heads on four occasions. That does not mean that the probability on any one spin is four in five or 0.8. If it is done much longer, say for 50 times, it will come out very close to a 25:25 split. The more often an event occurs, the closer the cumulative results will be to the probability.

The use of all this to the manager is that he is unwise to forecast solely on the basis of instinct. Take the example of a development manager responsible for a new piece of equipment which uses a lot of unproven technology. It consists of 100 modules, each of which has worked in test conditions 19 times out of 20. Thus, he concludes, the probability of failure of each module is only one in 20. It hardly seems worth working out what the probability is of the whole assembly working, but just for fun he does so. He multiplies the 0.95 probability of each of the 100 modules working satisfactorily, thus:

$$0.95^{100} = 0.006$$

To his surprise he finds that the probability of the equipment working is 0.006, or six chances in 1000. This happens because the cumulative risk of one chance in 20, taken over 100 modules, is so great.

He rushes back to the drawing board, and raises the reliability of the modules. Also, he halves the number of modules of which the equipment is made up. Testing shows that the probability of failure of each module has now fallen from 0.05 to 0.02; thus, the probability of each working has risen from 0.95 to 0.98. Using the new number of 50 modules, the calculation of probability of the equipment working is:

$$0.98^{50} = 0.36$$

It is still a very unreliable piece of equipment; the probability of its working is only 0.36, or about one time in three. Nevertheless, it is a great advance on six chances in 1000. It would be just a small step to turn the calculation on its head to discover what combinations of reliability and number of modules would achieve a probability of an acceptable level of reliability. To stick with the 50 modules, if the reliability of the equipment is to rise to a probability of working of 0.95, the probability of each module working will have to rise to around 0.999, or one failure in 1000.

Distribution

Distribution records how events are distributed among a range of categories. They can concern frequency and probability.

A frequency distribution can be illustrated by people's shoe sizes. A few have very large or very small feet, and the majority are around the average. In statistical terms, there is a low frequency distribution of small and large sizes, and a high frequency of average sizes.

Figure 2 shows a histogram or bar chart portraying an imaginary frequency distribution of shoe sizes, based on a sample of 10,000 women.

A distribution such as the one shown in Figure 2 makes it easy for the manufacturer and shopkeeper to see the right mix of sizes to make and to stock. In other words, recording of the frequency distribution has produced the basis for prediction. It is no great problem to see how the raw figures can be converted into probabilities, so that people not ordering 10,000 pairs at a time could also get their mixes right. Converted from a frequency distribution into one showing probability, the picture is as shown in Figure 3.

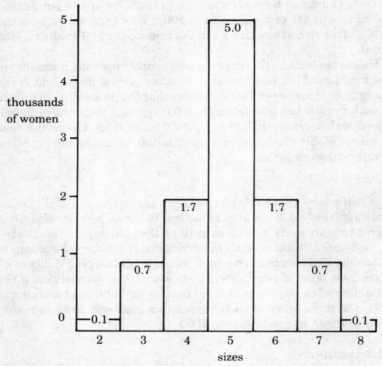

Figure 2 *Hypothetical distribution of shoe sizes*

The retailer and manufacturer can see that half of their production and stock probably ought to be in size 5, since the probability is that any customer will be of that size. Alternatively, he might decide that he will ignore the 'tails' of the distribution, sizes 2 and 8, where he stands to make only 2 per cent of his sales: they could be more trouble than they are worth. That would imply that more than 50 per cent of the stock ought to be in size 5, and so on for the remaining sizes. Alternatively, he may feel that every other supplier cuts out the unpopular sizes, leaving a useful market segment of neglected consumers which he could specialise in. Then again, he could remember that a lot of his trade in smaller sizes comes not from adults but from schoolchildren, and decide to beef up his order of the smaller sizes.

Whatever decision the shoe trader takes is of no importance to us. What is of concern here is that statistics and statistical methods have yielded information to help decisions. In no case has the

Figure 3 *Probability distribution from Figure 2*

distribution effectively dictated the decision, but instead it has provided food for thought and a jumping-off point for its user to decide what to do. Because he had the information the decision will be of higher quality than it might otherwise have been.

The same sort of technique can be used in all kinds of business activities. An example is in quality control. Huge efforts can be made to eliminate faults which are very infrequent and easy to remedy. A look at the probabilities and frequency distributions is likely to prompt the useful thought of whether it might be better to cure the problem when it arises, rather than cutting out at much higher cost any chance of its happening at all. It can also help when deciding which slow-selling products in a range to discontinue and which to drop. In one case statistics can help to show how often the infrequent failure is likely to arise, and in the other, to show whether sufficient market exists to justify the effort of trying to sell more.

Hunch could have come to the same conclusion, but it is a poor basis for such decisions.

The next move is to look in more detail at distributions. The measure of shoe size proceeds in clear steps, because that is how shoes are made. If instead the measure had been the length of feet, the steps between sizes would have been all but indistinguishable. In place of the steps on the histogram there would have been a curve. A distribution of that sort is called 'continuous'.

The continuous distribution which occurs most in nature and in human activity is known as the 'normal' distribution. Normal distributions come in all sorts of sizes, but they all have in common the same bell-curve shape. It might be tall and narrow, or wide and flat, or tall and wide and so on. Figure 4 shows two typical profiles.

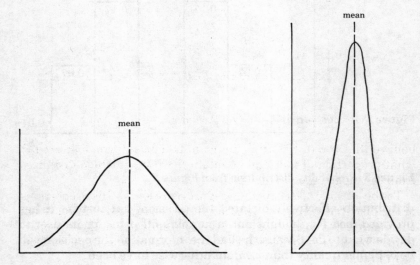

Figure 4 *Two typical normal distributions*

The shape of the distribution is expressed by two parameters: the mean (in everyday terms, an average), and the standard deviation (which is calculated to a formula which scientific calculators and personal computers have installed in them). Normal distributions always have the same form. This means that, of the total area under the curve, there is always the same proportion at a given distance from the mean. That distance is measured in standard deviations. So, if you have a mean and a standard deviation, and

Figure 5 *Proportions and standard deviations*

believe that the distribution ought to be normal, you can predict what proportion of the total population will lie at which distances from the mean, as in Figure 5.

To the left side of the mean in Figure 5 are shown the proportions of the distribution at one, two and three standard deviations from the mean; to its right are shown the accumulation of those proportions. The same information can then be taken one stage further, as in Figure 6.

Figure 6 shows that at one standard deviation on either side of the mean, 68.26 per cent of the population is represented. If the distance from the mean is doubled to two standard deviations, the proportion covered rises to 95.44 per cent. Thus, all but 4.56 per cent (100–95.44) is covered at just two standard deviations from the mean. Since that is so close to 95 per cent, the question might well arise: how far from the mean do I have to go to cover that proportion? A glance at the standard tables will show it to be at 1.96 standard deviations on either side of the mean.

The practical use of this distribution is great. To return to the earlier example of shoe sizes. The normal distribution supplies

95

Figure 6 *Proportions either side of the mean*

answers to such questions as: What proportion of consumers take (say) size six or more? What proportion of the market is satisfied by (say) the three most popular sizes? In essence, where is our time best spent? All are questions of considerable importance to the manufacturer and retailer alike. The distribution's use is not confined to the broad marketing issues: it can be applied to orders received, customer patterns, stock items and time spent, as well as many more besides.

The great truth which the normal distribution uncovers is that there is a disproportionate reward for effort spent in different ways. One standard deviation to both sides of the mean covers only one third of the width of the distribution, which is to say one-third of the ways in which you spend your time and effort. Yet that third of your time yields more than two-thirds (68.26 per cent) of the results. Apply it to many activities and it will show that a third of the work produces two-thirds of the results. Whether or not the distribution is normal will govern the applicability of this proportion in any given case. The overall message remains: a minority of activity produces most of the output. From there it is not a great leap to conclude that managers need to do two things, repeatedly advocated throughout this book: to minimise or discard entirely relatively unproductive activity, and to increase the share of their time and effort given over to the work that really gets the results.

One thing to remember is that the normal distribution does not cover 100 per cent of the population, just 99.74 per cent, so that the curve never quite touches the base line. It is not vitally important in most practical situations, but it should not be forgotten. Thus none of the predictions which are made from a distribution is ever completely accurate. This is not the place to go into detail, but forecasts made by these means should always be expressed as subject to a degree of uncertainty. The specialist textbooks go into these issues and supply the formulae; and most database and spreadsheet programs for personal and home computers will do the calculations automatically.

So far we have dealt with distributions in which the characteristics of the whole population are known. Frequently, in real life, that is not the case; we have information on only a few items, and would dearly like to predict the characteristics of the population at large. Again, distributions are a useful tool.

The first principle is that any samples we obtain from the population must be truly random. The statistician's definition of randomness is quite specific: each member of the population as a whole must have an equal chance of being picked.

Once the sample is assembled, it is important to know how well it represents the whole. That is largely a question of its size, not of what proportion it is of the total population. As a rough guide, 30 to 40 is usually the minimum for most purposes, though it is calculated exactly for a given confidence level. The more confident you want to be, the larger the sample must be. Thus questions of cost come in, since bigger samples cost more to deal with, both in time and money. One standard technique which has emerged from sampling techniques is the quality control chart.

Quality control charts
If a machine makes thousands of items, it is impossible – or, at least, extraordinarily expensive – to test each one for conformance to quality standards. Thus some form of sampling is the only realistic way of checking. But that sampling has to be sufficiently representative of the whole output to make the exercise mean anything.

To produce a Quality Control Chart (QCC), the ideal has to be defined first. That might relate to a dimension: say, a diameter. It is specified as a given size, plus or minus an amount known as 'tolerance'. (Sometimes tolerance runs one way only, so that, for example, an item may be of a certain size or greater, but no less.) Next, the size of sample to be taken in order to conform to the required confidence-level is calculated. Two limits have thus been defined: the warning limit, which, if a sample exceeds it, triggers a further investigation to increase the degree of certainty of the information; and the action limit which, if exceeded, causes the machine to be stopped, reset and re-started. Where the tolerance is expressed as plus-or-minus, the QCC will look like Figure 7.

Figure 7 *Quality control chart*

In Figure 7, the first three checks, taken at exactly half-hourly intervals, showed that the samples' averages were not of the target size, but none was outside the warning limit. The fourth check showed that the warning limit had been exceeded. That resulted in further checks, not shown on Figure 7, which proved this to be a rogue result. Thus, on this occasion the machine was not stopped and costly down-time was avoided. The action to be taken at each stage is very much up to the manager responsible to decide, the important part of the message being that the degree of tolerable deviation can be calculated, as can the size and frequency of sampling necessary to give an acceptable substitute for testing the entire output.

98

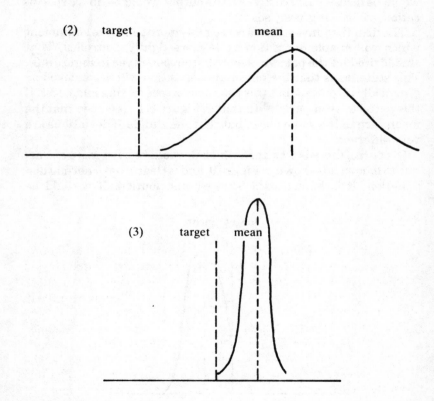

Figure 8 *The effects of different normal distributions*

Distribution: some further examples

A firm makes rather expensive gold-contact switches for specialist electrical applications. The amount of gold deposited on the contacts is critical to both costings and quality. Too little gold and the contact will not perform, too much and the product makes a loss. The firm believes that the variation follows a normal distribution, and is trying to define its quality specification for gold deposits.

It is possible for the pattern of gold deposition to follow the distribution in Figure 8(1). That would be a quality disaster: a very large proportion of the output would fall below the target size.

Following the same pattern of distribution, the firm moves the mean well above the target size, as illustrated in Figure 8(2). That clears it of practically all risk of making the deposits too small, but would be disastrously costly. All the output would be above specification, some of it grossly so.

The firm then investigates some new, more sensitive equipment which will enable deposition to be more tightly controlled. That should produce the pattern of distribution portrayed in Figure 8(3). This still means that the minimum deposition will be achieved by practically all output, but this time at excesses costing much less. If this pattern is compared with that in Figure 8(1), it is seen that the means are in the same place, but that the standard deviations are very different.

Of course, there is a pattern which it would be even more attractive to follow. It is shown in Figure 9, and is clearly not a normal distribution. It is known as a 'skewed' distribution. If it could be

Figure 9 *A skewed distribution*

achieved, it should ensure both that no product falls below the minimum standard, and that the least excess occurs above the minimum.

Despite its asymmetrical shape, formulae exist to calculate such distributions as this, just as they do for the more regular shape of the normal distribution and its close relatives.

Regression and correlation

So far, questions involving only single variables – height, weight and so on – have been addressed, which can be arranged into one distribution or another. Other types of problems exist, in which more than one variable is at work.

Often in problems of this sort patterns are sought as aids to understanding. As an example, a farmer feeds his animals to make them gain weight. The faster they do this, the sooner they can be sold and new ones be brought in, and the greater will be the return on his land, buildings and labour. He is therefore very interested in this question. He experiments, and produces a chart, shown in Figure 10.

Figure 10 *Linear regression*

101

The dotted line in Figure 10 is the 'line of best fit', and is not sketched in by eye. It is calculated by the process of regression analysis. Where one straight line is involved, it is known as linear regression.

Usually it is not enough merely to fit the line to the results. One also wants to know how good the fit is; that involves calculating the correlation coefficient. Where it is equal to one, the fit of the line to the points on the chart is perfect. Where it is lower it shows how close to – or distant from – a perfect correlation there is between the two factors under consideration.

Frequently there are more than two factors at work. In the case of the animal feeding example there most certainly are. The extent of veterinary care, the mix of foodstuffs, health, the use of growth additives, the weather, the availability of drink, access to shelter, the extent of exercise – all have their influence, as well, probably, as many more.

The farmer is clearly concerned to know more about this, as he does not want to give £2-worth of food to make up for a temperature drop that it would have cost £1 to remedy.

The technique used to relate all these factors is multiple regression. In this case it reveals the optimum mix of inputs to achieve the best output before diminishing returns start to set in. To show all of the factors listed above would make for a very confusing illustration, so just one other factor appears in Figure 11, the temperature in the creatures' housing. A very low temperature results in poor weight gain, as the animals use too many calories keeping warm; a high temperature depresses appetite and hence weight gain. Once again, the farmer's experiments do not explore the extremes.

The point A marks the spot at which the food and the temperature curves cross one another, in other words, where they start to cancel each other out. At that point they are in equilibrium, so that is the point at which the temperature and feeding rate are held.

As has been stated, multiple regressions can appear somewhat complicated. Figure 12 shows one such. Despite its appearance, its message is easy to see. If A is what we are trying to maximise (say, weight gain), level three on the B scale is where its highest level is reached. We therefore pitch all the other inputs at their level which corresponds with B at three. There is no point in putting in more, as it will not give a worthwhile result. In a sense, we are boxed in at that point.

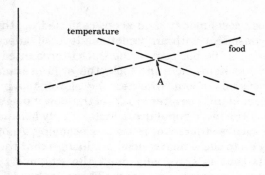

Figure 11 *Multiple regression with two factors*

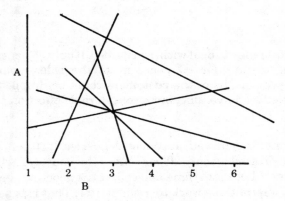

Figure 12 *Multiple regression with several factors*

Pareto's Principle, or the 80:20 rule

As has already been said, most of any effect is accounted for by a minority of the inputs. This rule takes that idea further. It states that – roughly speaking – 20 per cent of the work done will account for 80 per cent of the output; the other 80 per cent of the work can therefore produce only 20 per cent of the results.

Applied to managers' work in organisations, this idea is enormously powerful. Of course, the split is rarely exactly 80:20, but it is usually near enough for the message to be valid.

As examples, four areas will be taken: stock control, customers, vehicle journeys and a manager's personal time. The aim is to show how the 80:20 rule can help in each case.

103

Stock

Holding stock costs money, and keeps cash tied up; thus the bare minimum consistent with an acceptable level of safety is all that should be kept. If 80 per cent of the sales is accounted for by only one-fifth of the items held in stock, the organisation should be thinking seriously about whether the slower-moving products should be kept at all. Too often stocks of the slow movers are higher than those of the more popular products, simply because the same quantity of each is ordered for reasons of economy. Another reason for hanging on to these nearly dead products is that the customers expect it. If that is true, why don't the customers turn their supposed expectation into purchases? There can be valid reasons of this type, but tests of validity are rarely applied, the same old pattern being good enough for another year in far too many organisations.

Customers

It also costs money to deal with a customer. If only 20 per cent of the customers account for 80 per cent of the sales, some of the remaining four-fifths of the customers could be dropped with no noticeable effect on volume, but a considerable effect on costs.

Deliveries

It costs money to send vehicles out on deliveries. If 80 per cent of the output is delivered by only 20 per cent of the journeys, why bother with the rest? Let them come and collect the goods, or, better still, take their unprofitable work to a competitor. That rids us of a cost and imposes it on him, giving us a double advantage.

Manager's time

The manager's time is his key resource. Some would say that it is the only one that really matters. If 20 per cent of his work produces 80 per cent of his results, he clearly ought to throw overboard, quite ruthlessly, some of the things he does now, so as to free time for the really productive aspects of his work.

To take that point a little further, if he were to cut out the bottom fifth of the things he does, he would double the time available to tackle the work that produces 80 per cent of the results. While that does not mean he will immediately produce 160 per cent of the earlier performance, he could quite reasonably look for an increase in his effectiveness of 30, 40 or 50 per cent.

The opportunity of such huge improvements is not to be sneezed at. However, there may be problems when he tries to free himself from the cloying grip of relatively useless work. The notion of 'satisficing' comes in useful here. Satisficing involves intentionally setting out to do the bare minimum necessary, and absolutely no more. Applied to the less important work in a manager's life it frees large chunks of time, as well as avoiding the charge that he ignores parts of his duties altogether. The savings in time can be quite staggering: if it takes ten minutes to do a minor report quite roughly, it could take an hour to polish it to near-perfection. By satisficing, the wise manager spends 50 minutes of that precious hour on really important work, while his less discriminating colleague spends all of it on an unrewarding task.

Microcomputers

Since the early 1980s, a number of computer-based tools have become available to help the manager to do his job better. Not only can enormous amounts of brain-numbing routine be performed more or less automatically, but also things can now be done which were previously, in practical terms, impossible. Analyses and comparisons which the manager needed for next week were theoretically possible, but since gathering the information and processing it would have taken a month, they were never undertaken. The big, central computer of the 1960s and 1970s might have helped a little, but the combination of its inflexibility, its more or less permanent dedication to running payroll and invoicing routines, and the need for expert intermediaries, limited its helpfulness. The advent of the personal machine freed the individual manager from many of these limitations. The personal computer (PC) imposes its own, irksome, disciplines which can be hard to live with. That is especially true when the PC is replacing a familiar manual system.

The three software tools which have done most to change managers' lives are the word processor, the spreadsheet, and the database.

Word processors are basically programs which enable typing on to a screen, prior to printing on to paper. The document on the screen can be edited – mistakes can be put right, blocks of text can be shifted around, different layouts can be tried – before the document is committed to paper. They are therefore particularly valuable to the amateur typist (a category which embraces almost all managers) as well as to those professionals who have to draft documents for alteration, and who have to produce many

105

documents which contain standard elements. An entire document can be saved on to the computer's storage medium, for calling up another day. Figures, text and graphics can be imported from other programs and other files.

Spreadsheets are tools for planning and calculation. Imagine a vast sheet of paper, divided into tens of thousands of squares, hundreds of columns wide and hundreds of rows deep. Text or figures can be written on any of the squares (or 'cells' as they are called). If the cells are not long enough for what you wish to enter, you can elongate them. Only a part of the spreadsheet will be shown on the screen at any time, but the screen can be moved instantly to look at another area at any time. If there is an area you want to keep an eye on to see what changes are happening as a result of what you are doing elsewhere, you can display that bit at one side of the screen while you work.

Beneath the surface of any cell you can write an invisible formula which tells the program what to display on the surface of that cell. These formulae can be simple, or extremely complex.

As a simple example of what can be done, a simple stock record will serve. The month starts with a certain stock of the product, some are used, and some more are delivered in. To arrive at the month-end result involves simple arithmetic, which becomes tedious when many products and deliveries are involved. The month-end figure this month then becomes the opening figure for the following month. The formulae take care of all the additions, subtractions and carrying forward. All the operator has to do is enter the figures: the calculations are done for him.

Spreadsheets are capable of far more sophisticated work than simple addition and subtraction, but even here they guarantee instantaneous and error-free results.

Databases are quite different again. They are the computer equivalent of a filing cabinet full of clever record cards. Record cards because that is exactly what they resemble on screen, clever because they will sort and calculate. A database carrying records of customers will show name, address, telephone number, contact names and various other details for each one. In a filing cabinet it is possible to keep them in alphabetical order, or in some sort of geographical categories, or in any other way. The problem comes when we want information in a different form from the way in which the cards are filed. If they are in alphabetical order, it takes ages to list them in descending order by quantity purchased last year, or especially by those with more than three sites and buying four products from us in amounts of at least £10,000 per year.

None of those analyses creates more than a few minutes' work for the database operator in giving the instructions, and the machine gets on with the work while he does something else. Moreover, it will do totals, subtotals and percentages (and means and standard deviations!) for each category, if asked.

A final point on computers is that the programs can be difficult to master. Many people have bought programs which did not really suit them (the different programs really are different) and only found out after many painful hours. Most managers who do not have a specialised bias in their work find that an integrated suite of programs is best. In that, the three programs (or more) are welded together, so that there is no problem in, for instance, getting a piece of your spreadsheet printed out in a word-processed report. Too many computer dealers are not truly trying to serve their customers' best interests. Some seem to take advantage of customers' ignorance, selling what it suits them to sell rather than what their customer ought to have. Theoretically, the customer can protect himself by using a consultant, but many are unreliable, others are boffins who sell their favourite program which needs a degree in computer science to operate, some are really mainframe (that is, big) computer programmers slumming it in the micro market (which they do not really understand or like), and some are tied up with suppliers in a way that may remain undisclosed. All of them, good and bad, are expensive.

The only defence which the poor buyer has is to find a friendly, competent helper, such as his organisation's in-house expert. In any case, he ought to educate himself to some extent. His local ITEC (government-launched training facilities), night school, magazines and other users will teach him a lot. Perhaps the most educational route of all is to acquire one of the popular home computers and learn some programming from the manual which comes with the machine. Knowledge thus gained must not be used to write programs for important areas of analysis at work; the amateur can cause more problems than he has heard of. It will, however, serve as an excellent introduction to the exacting demands, precise thought-patterns and huge power which even the lowliest micro possesses.

Written records

A final note in this chapter concerns the necessity for written records.

In organisations there is a need for actions and decisions to be recorded in writing and circulated to those affected. There is a further need for records of performance to be kept, for internal purposes. The law also imposes requirements for the creation and retention of accounting records going back over many years.

If little or nothing in these areas is recorded in writing, opinion will rule rather than fact. Recollection of agreements can vary alarmingly from one individual to another ('You said you *would*' – 'Oh no, I said I'd *try*'), even within minutes of the event. Thus good housekeeping dictates the creation and maintenance of written records.

There is a further aspect – of self-interest. The world being what it is, the first-time manager is particularly vulnerable if a senior manager chooses to protect himself by denying a commitment he made. It is the senior, trusted person's word against that of the new junior. The only way the first-time manager can protect himself from that form of ill-treatment is by producing a written record. An exchange of memoranda or letters is best. A scribbled note to your file, timed and dated, and written immediately after the event while recollection is fresh, is better than nothing.

Chapter 5
Marketing

Marketing: what it involves

'Marketing' is misused and misunderstood more often than practically any other word in common business use today. To many people it is a polite word for selling, perhaps with a little advertising and publicity thrown in. While selling, advertising and publicity are important elements in the marketing process, they certainly are not everything that is involved.

Marketing starts from a particular view of what a business is for. The marketing view says that it is there to satisfy customers' needs at a profit to itself. To do this, it has to find out what those needs are, design products and services which will answer them, and set about supplying them. That has to be done at a price which is high enough to recover costs and make profit, and low enough to get the right amount of work – not too much, nor too little. Along the way someone has to go out and tell customers that the goods exist, get the orders, deliver and install, get paid, and then carry out after-sales services.

Mention of after-sales service suggests that the relationship continues after the sale. So it should, for that is how customers, once attracted, remain hooked. It is a lot easier – and for 'easier' read 'less expensive' – to sell a second time to a satisfied user than for the first time to someone who does not know the organisation at all. Indeed, the marketing process is a loop, which can be described by the diagram in Figure 13.

Figure 13 shows the overall picture of customer needs and the organisation's characteristics marrying up to produce what the customer wants. Then the product is distributed to the customer and he is told about it. The process is a loop, for once the purchase is completed the customer will have new and different needs which

Figure 13 *The marketing process simplified*

could be satisfied profitably. They may be for service and spares, add-ons, and repeat orders for new installations.

Listening to the market

A properly sensitive system for listening to customers' requirements will identify such opportunities. They will be spotted when the organisation hears the answers to such questions as:

- do the customers think we are doing better or worse than last year?
- do the customers think our competitors are doing better or worse than last year?
- what are we, and they, doing right?
- what are we, and they, doing wrong?
- how can we improve?
- what ought we to improve?

That list is only a summary, but it is a good place to start from for the organisation seriously interested in tracking its reputation among customers. From that simple list will flow many subsidiary questions. It may be difficult for the first-time manager to grasp it in his early days, but even the most high-faluting market research is really trying to find the answers to basic and simple questions like these. It is difficult because some people seem to think it necessary to surround what they do with as much mystery as possible. If the first-time manager cannot see what sense there is in what is said, he should ask what it means. Far from being thought a fool, he will earn the gratitude and admiration of others present for they, too, had not understood, but did not like to ask.

Few organisations bother to organise their information flows in a disciplined and planned way. Those who fail to do so risk heavy penalties, for the organisation that does not listen to its market loses touch with it; and an organisation out of touch with its market is a classic candidate for failure. The market is constantly evolving, fragmenting, changing its pattern and coalescing again. To keep up with all this the organisation needs information.

The place of marketing

Thus the role of marketing is central to the conduct of the business of any organisation, public, private or charitable. If an organisation fails to satisfy its customers' needs at a profit it will eventually fail altogether. If it fails to identify its customers' needs it has no real chance of satisfying them; and if it does not follow the evolution of those needs it will become increasingly out of touch and eventually irrelevant.

The term 'profit' may seem to sit oddly with mention of charities and some public bodies. To them, profit might not be expressed financially, but in terms of a movement towards their objectives. It might be recognised as cleaner streets, more families helped, or an important building saved. The benefits to the organisation are impossible to express financially, but benefits they are, and they can be described as profits. Certainly, viewed as profits, they make sense in marketing terms.

The information gathered by the marketing function is not just interesting; it will influence – or it ought to – the organisation at all levels. If the organisation normally deals with its customers via dealers, and finds that instead it ought to deal with them direct, the

111

resulting change will be felt by virtually everyone. Top management will have to develop new ways of assessing trends, for they will no longer be able to rely on their dealers to tell them what is happening, the accounts department will suddenly have to process thousands of small payments rather than a few big ones, the pattern of deliveries will change, with effects on the people concerned. In the sales department's hierarchy, the king will be toppled. Previously it was the person who supervised the dealers: they had to be kept happy or there were no sales. Now he is supplanted by the person who is expert in direct-selling techniques.

The whole strategy and direction of the organisation has to be market-led. Production, distribution and administration policies must be strongly influenced by marketing considerations. Staff selection and training have to take marketing into account, or else the telephone may be answered rudely and the delivery drivers look scruffy. Even at the lowest level of detail marketing obtrudes: the look of the company's letterhead and the decision over which grades of paper to use for which correspondence can, in some circumstances, be very important.

Marketing people

Really good marketing people have to possess a wide range of strengths and characteristics. Indeed, they need to be among the most versatile of managers. The reason is that they are required to possess the skills and gifts of numeracy, an informed literacy, aesthetic sense and an understanding of people and their behaviour which is at the same time both instinctive and rational.

Numeracy is necessary to deal with statistics and management accounting concepts. The marketing managers' literacy does not just mean the ability to read and write, but the ability to express himself well and persuasively as well as to understand the written work of others such as advertising and PR people. Design, both graphic and three-dimensional, is very important in marketing, and the aesthetic sense to distinguish good from bad is vital. Probably the most fundamental is the understanding of people, for it is their motivations which decide, in the end, whether or not the organisation's products are bought and appreciated.

Often we think of people as being good with figures but not aesthetically minded, or full of insight into people but hopeless with figures. This is probably because most of us play to our strengths, developing the things we are already good at. Marketing managers, or the good ones at least, cannot afford to be like that. They realise that they have to be good at every part of their diverse work, and train themselves accordingly.

The combination of many areas of competence in one individual may suggest examples from another age. Renaissance man was master of the sciences as well as the arts of his day. He understood and could perform the detailed, meticulous accumulation of evidence, the formulation of hypotheses and their testing, proceeding the while by a series of mostly small steps, each secured by the certainty of absolute proof which the scientific method demands. By an infinity of such steps the whole of today's science was created.

But Renaissance man did not stop there. He was interested in everything. Not for him the grudging attitude of some scientists, summed up by the great Lord Kelvin in words to the effect that, if you cannot measure it, your knowledge is not really worth having.

In marketing, too, there is a place for both art and science. As in life generally, in marketing science cannot explain everything, and is plumb useless in approaching some issues. Scientific method must be used where it can contribute to understanding, but it cannot replace judgement. Rather, an educated judgement trained by experience is king, and uses the information provided by scientific methods as one element in its fuel. Otherwise every chief executive would be a PhD, highly qualified in a narrow field.

In marketing, as elsewhere, it is important to know when to seek scientific information and when to apply judgement. The analytical side of marketing is extensive, but it does not outweigh the interpersonal and creative aspects. Marketing needs new ideas: they can be prompted by information and analysis, but someone has to apply the vital spark of creative intelligence to bring the new idea into being. Marketing research never does more than provide the information which is the launching pad for ideas. Current techniques are not up to having the ideas as well. The emergence of computer-based 'expert systems' could change that picture dramatically.

The people side of marketing is important too. As well as in their role as colleagues, marketing practitioners encounter people as customers, both individual and in the mass. That statement could be challenged on the ground that the mass is no more than a collection of individuals. So it is, in one sense. But if the behaviour of single individuals is studied it yields less information than if attempts are made at categorisation as well; categorisation involves aggregation into masses.

Marketing and communication

The colleagues with whom marketing people deal are both internal and external. Those in their own department and elsewhere in the organisation participate in conventional colleague relationships. To refer to suppliers such as advertising, PR and research agencies as colleagues may seem odd, if the special nature of relationships with them is not appreciated. Those agencies are much more than mere suppliers; they immerse themselves in the ethos and values of the organisation in order to understand it as well as possible. Indeed, one very well known shoe company was built on the basis of technology supplied by the machinery manufacturer and marketing direction supplied by the advertising agency, and that is far from being the only case of a significant contribution coming from such sources.

Marketing's dealings with customers and consumers are central to its concerns. (Customers – such as shops – buy from the manufacturer or other supplier; consumers are the end-users. Tesco is Lever's customer. The member of the public who buys Persil from Tesco is the supermarket's customer and Lever's consumer. It is perfectly possible for the customer to be the consumer as well, where the consumer is supplied direct by the manufacturer.) Marketing studies people individually in some depth, in order to discover how their minds work in general, and in particular how they react to particular propositions. The large collection of individuals which constitutes the mass is also studied for signs of opportunities to create groupings. Those groupings should highlight opportunities for, or threats to, the organisation. For example, a clear indication that a product suitable for all age-groups is popular only with the old is an obvious danger signal for the future of that product. Or the emergence of a group with needs which are at present unsatisfied might be seen, and products or propositions designed for them. Such groups are called 'segments'.

The appreciation of aesthetics may seem to be a strange item to add to a list of desirable qualities in a marketing person. Its relevance is that aesthetics is an important element in communication, and communication is one of marketing's main areas of concern.

Words are one important medium of communication. The marketer deals with them in many forms, most notably perhaps in research reports, recommendations for action, advertising copy, instruction manuals, and letters to users (especially the dissatisfied ones).Anyone unable to appreciate well-written examples of these forms of communication is ill-qualified for marketing work. He does not have to be able to write well himself – though it would help – but he has to be able to recognise good, and bad, writing when he sees them.

Visual images are another tool of communication. An eye for an image which works is essential (questions of beauty or ugliness are irrelevant here: the criterion is whether or not the right message is conveyed well). To appreciate a particular image's effect fully, he has to be aware of what its impact would be in other media and other styles. Thus he needs an understanding of the strengths and limitations of all visual media in order to be able to do his job well.

Every product has a three-dimensional form. Whatever its shape, it conveys messages to the observer about what it can and cannot do. Those messages ought to be the ones which the marketer wants to be received. Thus he needs some appreciation of the effect which three-dimensional design has on people. A spade may *be* strong, but if it *looks* weak where the blade meets the handle, people will not buy it. A scent-bottle may hold the product quite securely, but if it reminds people of a jam jar it is unlikely to sell. An electric drill that appears to have been fathered by a rhinoceros looks as if it can survive the toughest of jobs.

To acquire these skills the marketer does not have to gain degrees in fine art, design, literature and sculpture. The more he studies the visual image, the three-dimensional object and the way that words work, the better he will be at some parts of his job. He will be better able to understand and be understood by the specialists with whom he works, and he will probably increase his appreciation of something which has pleased civilised man through the ages.

It is essential that marketing personnel are at least competent in their dealings with people. They have to work with advertising agencies, PR firms, and a wide range of people from both within and outside the organisation. To make sense out of that challenge, marketing personnel have to be sensitive and sympathetic, with some insight into people's feelings, drives and emotions. Furthermore, because they have to make abstract concepts understood, they need to be able to express themselves well. Leadership characteristics are also called for: advertising and PR people work best when they are motivated and excited about the opportunity to advance their careers by working on the organisation's account. Sometimes these creative people have to be told that their work is not acceptable, and told in such a way that they really want to do it again and better.

The pressures in marketing

When someone is placed in such an exposed and demanding position they can feel extreme pressure to perform. They often have to pull together a new campaign in a hurry, with insufficient time for thought and consideration. Its results become obvious quite quickly, and even if it is a success nobody awards bouquets; they just keep their jobs a little longer. Success is expected, and perhaps overtly demanded. After a success everyone looks ahead to the next campaign, expecting it to be even more effective.

The constant pressure which this imposes leads to all sorts of problems. Individuals get the sack, or suffer breakdowns trying to avoid it. Many change jobs frequently. That does neither them nor their employer much good. People who job-hop never stay in one place long enough to build a record of real contribution. They are more like primitive hunter-gatherers, flitting from one set of pickings to another, than the farmers who stay put and improve the soil and yields year after year. Organisations which stimulate job-hopping ask for the trouble they get. If they press for more and more immediate results they have only themselves to blame if staff deliver a quick fix of achievement and then move on. Often they have to, for they know that the chickens have taken off and are already on their way home to roost. The organisation suffers because no continuity of experience is built up in the marketing department, and the newcomers are rarely able to make much impression on their battle-scarred colleagues from other departments.

Some individuals survive the process and the best rise rapidly to positions among the élite MDs of major companies. Those who do not make the grade are not all duffers, and many go on to exercise their skills in marketing services companies, in consultancy and training, often by starting their own businesses.

The marketing task

Planning
Like all management functions, marketing has long-, medium- and short-term aspects and perspectives. They can be described as in Figure 14.

Long-term:	5–10 years	identify likely needs of the market, and how to satisfy them at a profit
Medium-term:	1–3 years	set up the practical implementation of long-term ideas
Short-term:	up to 1 year	practical implementation: getting sales, controlling costs, making profit

Figure 14 *Long-, medium- and short-term marketing perspectives*

The process of planning these events does not take place just once every five or ten years, of course. Most organisations have 'rolling' plans which, every 12 months, move forward by one year. Any organisation with any sense will not stick too rigidly to its planning cycle: a good idea or a new opportunity which appears unexpectedly will not be shelved for up to five years just because it was not thought of at the right point in the planning cycle.

The plans of the marketing department are one element in the total plan for the organisation as a whole, the corporate plan. Other departments will submit their plans for finance, production and personnel, but none of them can really get going before the marketing plan is ready. A production plan which proposes levels of output for which there is as yet no sales forecast is rather pointless. Once some sort of sales forecast has been made, production people can get to work properly on their own planning.

Likewise, the personnel department cannot plan to train or recruit particular skills until they know what skills are wanted, in what quantity and when. They cannot decide whether or not to replace people who retire until they know if that contribution will still be needed.

Finance, too, has to await marketing and production plans. Once it knows the likely timings and size of cash flows it can consider whether the outflows are temporary or permanent, and thus how they should be covered. There is only one major exception to that principle. It occurs where the organisation's finances are likely to be under stress. In such cases the financial people will publish in advance the constraints which have to be imposed on stocks and sales. Their colleagues can then work within those limits, saving time, trouble and friction.

The way in which the marketing department goes about its task of long-term planning is a combination of the usual ingredients: science, intuition and judgement. A generalised view of the process is offered in Figure 15.

117

Figure 15 *Strategic marketing planning*

Information for the planning process

The materials which the marketer uses in this process are largely provided by others. Economists analyse trends and forecast what will have happened to people's and industries' power and propensity to spend in future years. Some industries will have disappeared altogether and new ones will have arisen. Much of that work is speculative, but if it takes ten years to build the power station you need to know by 1990 at the latest whether or not it is likely actually to be needed in the year 2000. Some long-range forecasting may be bordering on guesswork (albeit informed), but if there is no other source of independent evidence it must not be ignored altogether. Of course, the forecasters' ideas are not swallowed uncritically, but are modified by personal intuition and judgement.

Demographic forecasts are on safer ground. They deal with the composition of the population. In 1988 it is easy to say how many children aged between 13 and 16 there will be in the year 2000, for all of them have been born. Applying a known factor for child mortality has always produced a very reliable forecast until now. The emergence of AIDS has thrown such forecasting into disarray. On the evidence of past epidemics and pandemics, it will not be the last unexpected factor suddenly to appear.

Forecasts of lifestyle have always existed, but more attention has been paid to them of late. The idea behind them is that the products and services which people choose to buy are part of a package which, in total, can be described as a lifestyle. The marketer's task is to identify the lifestyles of different groups and to find out two things: unsatisfied needs, and ways of positioning the organisation and its products to match them to the group's view of itself. An early – and by now universal – example of an obscure product which became a mass market lifestyle item is blue jeans. Originally a manual worker's workwear, it gained glamour by association with the American cowboy and hence became the uniform of youth in the 1950s and 1960s. Today, lifestyle marketing is concerned with finer divisions, hence the consciousness of groups like Yuppies, who are on the receiving end of targeted promotion of cars, drinks, clothes, furniture and many other items. Perhaps the ultimate irony is that members of these groups believe that wearing the uniform that defines membership is an expression of their individualism.

Thus there is a great deal of information on the population at large lying around, just waiting for the marketer to pick it up. That which cannot be located from existing sources can be acquired by various techniques which split into two categories: quantitative and qualitative.

Marketing research

Quantitative research, as the name suggests, deals with quantities and numbers, things that can be counted. It seeks to establish how many of us do, have done or will do (or not do) a particular thing, such as buy anti-dandruff shampoo. It is mostly conducted via interviews or questionnaires. From the aggregated results of all the answers given, the researcher can form a picture of how a market is made up. If the same research is repeated at intervals, change and the direction it takes can be monitored.

Qualitative research deals with the feelings which people have about their needs, and about products, services, and organisations. By definition it cannot, and does not try too hard to, apply numbers to its findings. It can give a vivid impression of the views that people hold and the issues which they consider to be important. It is often conducted by the *Group Discussion method*, under which a number of people – up to 10 or 12, usually – talk about an issue, guided by an experienced leader. The participants are carefully selected to represent a particular group which the organisation is interested in.

119

Often an organisation will use the two broad categories of research to complement one another. Qualitative research establishes the issues which people seem to find important, and quantitative information is gathered to test the true representativeness of the views expressed.

One error which inexperienced marketing people are prone to make is to become hypnotised by the apparatus, jargon and science of research. It is easy to believe that it provides all the answers they will ever need, and that nothing should be done unless there is positive research support for it. For one thing, research needs interpreting. For another, it can only ever report on what is. It can never synthesise ideas or exhibit flair, two of the marketing department's more important duties. Only a human being can discern from research reports the possible existence of an unfulfilled need, and design an imaginative answer to it.

Just as these techniques apply to consumer markets, so they are used to find out what industry wants. Industrial research starts with a great advantage, in one area at least. Organisations which sell to the public can foresee their own needs, using the research techniques described here. Suppliers to those organisations are able to use the same sources of information to adjust their own marketing effort. If the public taste shifts to new products, the factories which make them will need new equipment. Organisations supplying those factories with equipment can thus see what they will need to do – but only if they take the trouble to keep abreast of the information available.

Even for pure industrial companies, far removed from consumer markets, information is abundant. Even if, at first glance, it is not apparent it is often in existence or can easily be generated. In industrial marketing especially, it is frequently unnecessary to build a better mousetrap; giving quicker delivery or better after-sales service can be the key to swinging the market your way.

Advertising

What advertising is for

For many people the world of advertising seems glamorous. Quite why this should be is a mystery, but it may have something to do with that world's ability to spin dreams out of next to nothing. For advertising is simply a tool for doing a job, just like any other technique employed in marketing.

The job of advertising is to spread a predetermined message in a controlled way to a specified audience. It is under control insofar as the message, how it is expressed and where it appears are all dictated by the advertiser. (There can be exceptions, as when the alcohol advertisers can hardly get on to TV at Christmas because the government has booked all the best spots for its drink-driving campaigns.) Advertising is solely about communication, a vital element in any marketing activity. Because its place is so important in some markets, and because vast expense can be involved, it becomes a topic of great interest at senior levels of general management. It is quite normal for big-brand advertising campaigns to cost millions of pounds.

At the other end of the spectrum are those firms in which advertising plays little or no part. They find that their communication objectives are best met by other means; thus the creation and control of advertising are by no means important issues for every marketing manager. However, if a marketing manager lacks experience and understanding of advertising he is deficient, for circumstances can arise in which it could be the right tool for a particular job. Indeed, in recent years many organisations which were previously not engaged in advertising have started to employ it. Frequently they are the industrial suppliers who used to think that their sales force visits to customers and presence at exhibitions were all the effort necessary. More recently they have come to understand the way in which appropriate advertising can create a receptive atmosphere for the sales force, and pull more people on to their exhibition stands.

Advertising media

The main media available to the advertiser are:

- direct mail
- radio
- TV
- press
- cinema.

There are others – such as posters, directories and exhibitions – which have their own specialised uses. Posters can help in mass markets where constant awareness of the product is desired, usually in support of a campaign on other media. Exhibitions are an excellent way of contacting the really interested potential buyer, for few people waste their time and money going to exhibitions on subjects that they are not committed to.

Direct mail involves sending letters and other sales materials through the post. Its objectives can be various: to fix appointments for salesmen to call, to solicit enquiries for catalogues, to obtain an order, to invite people to a demonstration, or any of a number of aims. The characteristic of most direct mail advertising is that it asks for direct action – filling in a reply-paid card, making a telephone call, etc – and that its effect is readily measurable.

The other sorts of advertising hope eventually to result in buying action, but their immediate purpose is to inform and persuade. Here, radio may seem to be at a disadvantage to television, but as someone once said, the pictures on radio are better. The way in which radio can create mental images is far from fully exploited by advertisers. The medium suffers from three disadvantages at present: its largely localised impact, the nature of the audience which the commercial sector attracts and the creative content of its ads. The audience is primarily people who are at home during the day, and young people at other times. This prevents it from making the breakthrough into the popular consciousness which commercial TV has achieved. Too many of the ads are reminiscent of the early TV commercials' 'hard sell' and hectoring. If selling is a form of seduction, these ads seem to offer rape. They reflect the desperation of the double glazing firm anxious to get work in the summer, and the garden centre trying to shift the Christmas trees by 24 December. If that is the brief given to the advertising agency, small wonder that the ads seem uncomfortably strident. If advertising ever gets on to the mainstream stations of the BBC, delivering more of a mass audience uniformly across the country, the tone and effect could change markedly.

Press advertising is a far better developed form. It varies between the small classified ad in the special-interest magazine and a double-page spread in the Sun. Certain advertising tasks can be achieved only in press media. Its flexibility – from local and specialist media, through regional editions of larger publications, to full national coverage – is in its favour. So is its ability to deliver clearly defined segments of readers: well-off men, young women, etc. A further advantage is its life, as the reader can return time after time to a printed ad.

TV's great advantage is obvious: it moves and talks. It is a medium which is realistically available only to the larger advertiser, since the cost of time is high, and it is easy to spend up to six figures making the film itself. And the ads have to be repeated, for not everyone watches ITV all the time.

Cinema offers some of the advantages of TV but at lower total cost. However, the audience is made up almost entirely of young people.

Repetition of advertising has been touched on. It is a basic tenet of advertising that single ads rarely work. A fixation among marketing managers is the effort to measure and judge the degree of repetition necessary to achieve their communication objectives. A further consideration is the distinct creative opportunities offered by different media. The quality Scotch can be shown to advantage in a full colour magazine printed on art paper; the car can be shown in use on TV; and the excitement of the motor race will come over with great impact on the cinema screen. This can lead to the danger of stereotyped advertising: only a few of the ads for quality Scotch, for example, could be solely for the brand advertised. In many ads a different bottle could be substituted without causing a stir. Thus advertisers are constantly striving to convey their products' unique propositions in new and relevant ways. When it comes off, and it is consistent with all of the properties of the brand, it can raise a good product's sales performance into the super-growth league. In that way effective advertising not only sells more product, but it also supports prices against pressure for discounts, as well as building reputation which can be traded on in the future. The magic of it is that excellent advertising need cost no more than the mediocre variety.

Who creates advertising

Few organisations attempt to create their own advertising, except in the recruitment field. Even there specialised advertising agencies have grown up. Most product advertising is created by agencies, who usually buy the space or time in media as well. Media buying always used to be part of the full-service advertising agency activity, but specialised media buying organisations have grown up quickly in the last few years.

The relationship with the advertising agency is complex, can be difficult, and is potentially rewarding or disastrous. If marketing people seem to spend a lot of time with the agency it is not just because of the beautiful people and the superb hospitality. They are probably doing a great deal of valuable work. There is a lot at stake, both in the expenditure on advertising itself, and in personal reputation and career future. Most of the decisions are judgemental, and the scope for getting things wrong is therefore wide. Whilst an unexceptional campaign may just fail to win market share, it is possible to create a bad one which will lose it. Then the damage done is far wider than simply advertising budget down the drain.

Distribution channels

'Channels of distribution' is the marketing jargon for the route which an organisation's products and services take from the producer to the customer. In the case of most consumer products, the majority go via wholesalers and retailers. There is also a flourishing business done via mail order catalogues, as well as mail order direct from the maker to the user.

The various routes are summed up in Figure 16.

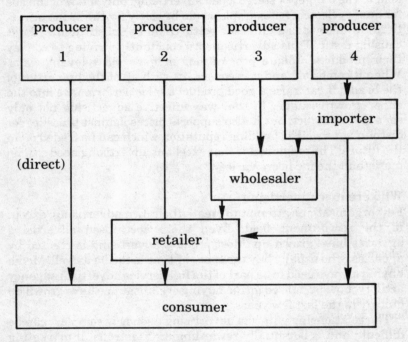

Figure 16 *Generalised view of channels of distribution*

In Figure 16 there are four producers, each with a different distribution policy. The picture given is representative of the options available, though there is nothing to stop organisations from adopting more than one channel if they wish. There can also be differences in nomenclature, such as the fact that wholesalers in the motor trade are called 'factors'. Then again, the retailer need not be a shopkeeper, but could just as easily be a mail order catalogue operator. Some wholesalers operate on full-service principles, others along cash-and-carry lines.

The choice of channels can be of great significance strategically. It sets the tone for many of the other marketing activities, as well as creating major constraints and setting up great opportunities.

One example of this effect will show its importance. If an organisation makes sweets, it has to decide how they will get to the shops so that the public can buy them. In only a few, specialised instances is that kind of product sold direct to the public, although sales direct to the catering trade may become important once the product's reputation is established. If it decides to sell through high-volume outlets it will have to create large-scale advertising campaigns, for unadvertised products are rarely stocked. Such is the competition for shelf space in these shops that evidence of advertising intentions alone will rarely be enough. Buyers will need to be convinced of the rightness of the marketing thinking behind the product before they will take it on. After all, the buyer's job is at stake, too.

An advertising-intensive firm needs a strong sales force to get, and keep, its products in distribution. It needs a good marketing department to give them the ammunition the salesmen need. Thus the firm becomes marketing, advertising and sales led, with obvious effects on its organisational shape and character.

Alternatively the firm could have decided to sell through low-volume outlets without advertising support. In that case, emphasis would be on product design, packaging, presentation at the point of sale, PR and salesmanship. Without advertising support, the way it looks in the shop determines whether or not it sells, and good salesmen are needed to get and hold distribution of unadvertised lines.

Another alternative open to the firm is to specialise in own-label manufacture. That would again change its character. There would be no advertising, perhaps some product and packaging design work, some selling at a senior level to just a few large outlets, and great emphasis on the control of costs and provision of service.

These three organisations are superficially the same: they are all confectionery manufacturers. But they will be very different places in which to work simply because of the diversity in their channels of distribution.

Selling and the sales force

Some people still persist in the belief that salesmen are born and cannot be made. It simply is not true. That supposition's only resemblance to fact is that it helps if would-be salespeople are naturally good at dealing with their fellow humans. Most sales managers prefer to recruit the less colourful but disciplined and trained salesman, than one whose ability stems solely from manner and charm.

Training is vitally important, for selling is a structured activity. Moreover, it has to be repeated frequently, since the salesman's skill deteriorates with the resistance he encounters. The general structure of a sale is described by the acronym AIDA, which summarises the stages through which every sale must pass. AIDA stands for:-

Attention: engaging the prospect's active attention in what is being said

Interest: relating the proposition to his problem

Desire: wanting the proposition on offer

Action: acting on that desire, placing the order.

While selling is an art, it is based on a body of theory and science, arising mainly from psychology. It needs all the help that it can get, for selling is a difficult task. It is concerned with getting someone else, voluntarily, to do what you want them to do.

The sales force, which has the job of putting those skills to work, may seem featherbedded. They are paid well, get company cars, expense allowances and incentive schemes. Office-bound colleagues may be heard to mutter that *they* don't need incentives to do their own jobs properly, so why does the sales force?

Two things are special about them. One is the competitive market for good sales people. If company A does not cherish them, company B will soon recruit them. If all the good people disappear in a short space of time, sales can fall sharply and drastically. Suppose one-third of orders stopped coming in: it throws finance, distribution and production into chaos. Losing key staff in any area of a firm can be hurtful, but rarely more so than in the sales force.

The second special factor is the conditions under which salesmen work. Not only are they under pressure to perform all the time, but unlike most of their colleagues they work alone. One of sales management's main headaches is keeping up morale while their people, frequently hundreds of miles from the company base, constantly experience rejection and frustration. A career in selling can be something of a paradox. Typically it attracts gregarious people, who then work alone and are constantly rejected. This presents sales management with some interesting challenges, and they find themselves permanently engaged in rebuilding damaged egos.

The two main reasons for employing a sales force at all are: 1. customers rarely buy things of their own volition, but tend to buy only what is sold to them; 2. the extra quantity that the salesman sells, not the amount which the customer might have bought anyway, is what justifies his costs.

Physical distribution

The way in which the product is conveyed to the customer touches on the interests of both marketing and distribution people. Typically, warehousing and distribution are part of the responsibility of the production department, but they ought also to be deeply affected by marketing considerations.

Where tangible goods are concerned, the first issue to be faced is who will be carrying the goods: a contractor or the firm's own transport? The former, as a specialist who might be recovering the cost of a journey from more than one customer, ought to be more economical; the latter is more easily controlled, will work more in the firm's interest and in some circumstances could be cheaper. The decision between these two courses has become less of a one-horse race in recent years, with the growth of a diverse range of transport services. Two decades ago, guaranteed 24-hour delivery was all but unheard of; now it is commonplace.

Marketing's concern with customer service ought to influence the choice of method and the standards to be observed in the distribution operation. Sometimes distribution can make all the difference to sales. If many firms offer delivery in four weeks, the organisation which switches to 48-hour waiting times ought to win. A close partnership between administration, production, warehousing and distribution will be necessary to make that turn from a promised breakthrough into a fact.

Product design

What the product or service does, how it does it and what it looks like are central marketing issues. They are also of no little interest to production people. Design ought to be based on:

- what the consumer's unfulfilled needs are known to be,
- what competitors are offering,
- what is feasible in technical and cost terms,
- the organisation's overall strategies.

To that list of ascertainable imperatives the designer brings personal flair. Everyone recognises flair when they see it, but defining it is not easy. Designers themselves say that it is rarely the result of a momentary flash of inspiration, but more usually it comes after many hours of disciplined thinking about the real nature of the technical, production and user problems involved. True insight is rarely instantaneous, and true insight is the stock-in-trade of every useful innovator.

Pricing, positioning and the marketing mix

Deciding how much to charge for the product is often thought of as an accountancy decision, but it should not be. The accountants are highly qualified to calculate a product's cost, and to explain the profit and cash-flow implications of a particular price, but they cannot set prices at all. The only relation which price (what it can be sold for) has to cost (how much it cost to make), is that it is preferable in most settings to see that the former exceeds the latter.

Pricing is a marketing issue, above all. It relates to what the customer wants, and how much he is prepared to pay for it. Nobody other than the marketing people have any idea of what that price is. They also know how they can maximise profitability by changing the product's 'positioning' and the 'marketing mix'.

Positioning has to do with the relationship between the product and its competitors. If the product is perceived by consumers as more or less the same as – or wildly different from – the competition, that ought not to have come about by accident. It should be as a result of a conscious marketing decision.

Marketers should be aiming for the maximum total profit. At a basic level, economics states that this can be achieved by selling a few at a high price or a lot at a low price, since demand falls off the more prices rise. The trick that the marketer tries to pull off is to defy the laws of economics. He wants to sell *more* at *higher* prices, for there real profit maximisation lies. Just putting up the price is rarely enough, though the mythology is full of stories of where a price increase was followed by a jump in sales. Usually other factors have to be adjusted too.

This is where the concept of the marketing mix comes in. It embraces all the attributes of the product itself and of the services surrounding it. It recognises that the proposition which the product presents is more than simply a bundle of functions, offered at a particular price. The extent to which any function is offered should come about, not by accident, but through calculation of consumer needs and the positioning it is intended to establish. Abstract values are included – indeed, they can be dominant in some markets – such as the tone of the advertising and where it appears, the style of the packaging, the perception of value relative to competition, the values which the product expresses, and many others besides. Crucial are the level, balance and effect sought from the various promotional expenditures.

To take a concrete example, contrast your own views of Fiat and Ford cars. Both are large, international companies with products for most market segments. How does each element in their propositions contribute to your perception of the two ranges of products? You may start off by thinking of the product itself, but before long you cannot avoid moving into considering intangibles. Which one has positioned itself better for you, and which one seems to have a mix of greater relevance to your needs? How has this come about?

Sales promotion

Sales promotion is a portmanteau term for all of those activities, with the exception of the sales force and advertising, which seek to influence demand for a product. Its most direct elements are limited-period offers to trade or user, and thereafter its link with the core activity becomes more tenuous, in the form of media publicity in editorial matter, sales force motivation schemes, sponsorships and charity deals.

The more competitive fields of business place much effort, expenditure and ingenuity into this field. To keep pace with competitors is their minimum requirement, to exceed them and excel is the aim. Agencies specialising in sales promotion work exist, for two primary reasons: few marketing departments can maintain the pace of innovation for very long, and the outsider's view can often bring more ideas to a jaded marketing department than it could ever generate for itself.

Trade relations

Largely the responsibility of the sales force, in this area they benefit from the support of publicists and promotional specialists. The trade can be reassured, just as much as a private individual, about a company and a product by means of favourable stories in the press. They may be harder-headed than the average citizen, but they are far from immune to influence.

The nature and scope of trade promotions are settled between sales (who have to implement them) and marketing (who pay). They both want long-term as well as short-term results, and at the very least do not want to run promotions which actually alienate the trade on which they depend – which has been done.

Public relations

Although PR has been touched on under a number of headings, it does deserve a section to itself since it has such potential to influence perceptions of organisations.

PR covers many activities, all directed towards two ends: improving perceptions of the organisation and its products among relevant groups, and limiting the extent of unfavourable perceptions when criticism is heard. Indeed, while most emphasis is placed on the constructive aspects of PR, its finest hour often comes when adverse stories are flying about. The trust developed with journalists in happier days then pays off, because the journalist telephones the PR person for *their* side of the story before filing his copy.

Contrary to popular opinion, the aspect of PR which deals with media relations is based not on lies and lunches, but on truth. That there can be many interpretations of the truth cannot be denied, but the good PR person never tries to deny facts.

To the regret of many PR people they sometimes have to deal in trivia, especially when dealing with the tabloid press. The more interesting aspects of the job for many are where they are negotiating to place senior people into interviews. Think of the eminent people (excluding politicians and trade union leaders) whom you have seen and heard on TV, and of the ones you know whom you have never seen. The difference is in both their attitude to publicity and the strength of their PR people.

PR also operates outside the media (though with half an eye on it). It seeks out influential groups who can help, or could cause trouble, and deals with them accordingly. A toy manufacturer, for instance, might try simultaneously to tell health visitors how its products help children to develop, and reassure consumer watchdogs about the care that goes into design and manufacture. It could also find itself called on to run a campaign aimed at Members of Parliament to persuade them against enacting unhelpful legislation.

Marketing: a summary

Marketing's position in the organisation is at the interface between its public and its own resources. It sets the agenda for the organisation, or at least it ought to. Everyone else in the organisation depends on the marketers to get it right, for without a market there can be no organisation.

Chapter 6
Managing Production and Services

Systems

Production is an important function, for if the output is not made there is nothing to sell. Making it is not enough: it also has to be available at the right time, to the right quality and at the right cost. Thus the main concerns of production managers are:

- Quality
- Quantity
- Cost – using the least inputs
  - carrying the lowest stocks possible
  - occupying the least space possible
- Timeliness.

As has been seen, the marketing department operates to a large extent with 'soft' systems (systems which are so complex that nobody can describe truthfully and fully the cause-and-effect relationships). For instance, why do people buy the product when and where they do? The influences governing such decisions are so complex and varied that they cannot be measured. As much as can be is measured, of course, but that still leaves many important quantities unknown. Therefore the manager has to fall back on judgement, which is the only realistic stance towards a soft system.

'Hard' systems, by contrast, are a lot easier to understand. They can be very complex, but what is going on is usually known and measurable. An example of a hard system is one for accounting. In a large organisation it may be extraordinarily complicated, but if you stop the clock at any point you can measure exactly what is in each account, what changes have taken place in a given period and why. Complex it may be, but a hard system is explicable and measurable.

As with an accounting system, so with a production control system. If 5000 items come in and 200 of them are rejected, 100 damaged in handling and 10 lost, 4690 must emerge from the other end. The facts of what happened in the journey from the goods-inwards bay to the finished goods store are known or are ascertainable.

Engineers are used to dealing with hard systems. The materials and processes which they manipulate have properties which are well known. For that reason, and because it is often an engineering environment, they tend to crop up in the production area. Frequently the production process throws up a large quantity of intricate detail for the manager to deal with, so that soft systems inevitably impinge on even the hardest system. An example is a volume car assembly plant. Hundreds of suppliers are responsible for delivering thousands of components; the requirement for the mix of output is constantly changing; different colours, trim requirements are called for from day to day. The output of that hard system is affected by all sorts of soft-system factors such as the rate of absenteeism. That can be determined by all sorts of influences, some predictable (like Cup Ties played away) and some less so (such as epidemics of influenza). Over time, experience will yield an average rate of absenteeism, but it does not always run true to past form.

Thus the total system which production represents is made up of a number of sub-systems – paint shop, raw material store, press shop, assembly line and so on. They in turn can be broken down into further sub-systems. Within the paint shop there is a section for preparation, another for applying the paint itself, a drying section, inspection procedures, and so forth. These can be broken down into individual job functions.

From this it will be seen that a map or family tree of the factory can be drawn. It starts with the complete factory, and subdivides it into progressively smaller functions. Or it could start from the bottom with the individual job functions, building up to the overall picture. Such a diagram would be very complicated, but the flows within it – of materials, labour and cash – would be known. For instance, it would never show electrical sub-assemblies travelling to the paint shop, or finished cars back-tracking to the press shop.

The predictability of the hard system means that, while there are millions of ways in which such a system could go haywire, producing the wrong things in the wrong quantities at the wrong time, the area in which the problem is being caused is identifiable.

Just as in the finished car itself, a malfunction in one sub-system (wheels and brakes, transmission, electrical etc) can cause faults in others and can be traced and put right.

People who are going to deal with this complexity need to possess analytical minds. They need great determination to keep things going whatever the problems, just like any effective manager anywhere. Unfortunately, the factory going quiet for an hour is more easily noticed than if the marketing department goes to pieces for a whole afternoon, so that their breakdowns are very public. Production managers also need to be numerate and good at the design and control of systems.

The kind of problems experienced in an advanced manufacturing environment operating under great pressure lend themselves to computer assistance. In keeping track of the complexity, working out the implications and even taking simple decisions, computers help a great deal. Stock control is an example of an area in which they contribute a lot. A retail chain trying to keep stocks as low as it can has a problem if it works from manual records of sales. The task of recording sales is laborious, then the delay between the information being available at the branch and being coordinated at HQ, and the working through of calculations of what has to be ordered, all takes time. Those delays mean that buffer stocks have to be held, just to cater for information processing. If instead sales are recorded at the checkout by computer, the information can be in HQ within seconds, processed into branch re-orders from the warehouse and, if necessary, replenishment ordered from the supplier. The only human intervention is to check that the firm really does want to re-order, just in case it is a seasonal line coming to the end of its life.

Hard systems which deal with great complexity and a great deal of routine processing of information are areas in which computer applications can thrive. They do the number-crunching chores, aggregate information, compare with performance criteria, and identify potential trouble-spots (such as potential stock-outs). Production managers are becoming increasingly computer literate as a result; they have to, and in any case they want to, in order to do their jobs better. The computer helps them to do their work better by helping them to spot where they are falling behind, and by meshing vast quantities of detail so as to replace estimation with measurements of results.

The management of people

In most organisations, the production function has traditionally employed the largest share of the workforce. The increasing application of automation to the production area has diluted this effect considerably in some industries, though for many it seems likely to remain true for some time to come. Thus its managers still need to possess skills in dealing with people. That does not mean that they are able to keep everyone happy all of the time, but it does mean getting the right results from them. For much of the time people may feel harassed if not actually overwhelmed, but if they can be shown how to cope and then to excel, past struggles will take on a rosy glow in retrospect.

Skills with people do not always come easily, to production managers or anyone else. If his upbringing is as an engineer, he has dealt with hard systems and with materials and processes with known properties. People are not like that. Their performance can vary, they can consistently under-achieve, and they can fail to show up altogether despite knowing that their contribution is vital. To someone who has been immersed in gears, motors, metals and hydraulics, these unpredictable creatures can be a real puzzle. One of three reactions seems to follow from that:

- surrender in confusion
- treat people like automata
- adapt.

The last is clearly the most desirable response, though many do seem to get stuck in the groove of the second option. Those who do, rapidly gain reputations as monsters. They have been known to get results, but under special circumstances, perhaps where people cannot afford to lose their jobs. That may be because their staff are paid very well or because there is little alternative work available. Even then their workforce can exhibit very high rates of turnover and loss. That in turn leads to high costs of recruitment and training, and permanently running at low efficiency. It is the best qualified who leave, and the least qualified who stay in such situations, so that the organisation becomes populated by the incompetent and the inexperienced.

In larger organisations trade unions will probably be represented. This is especially true in the public sector, where union membership is deeply entrenched. Indeed, most public-sector employees may not approach their managers over pay and

135

and conditions issues, since agreements exist which allow them to be the subject of discussion solely between management and unions.

The personnel department may contain specialists in negotiation, but they cannot operate without a production manager to tell them what to negotiate about, within what constraints and with what objectives. Even then the production manager cannot leave the personnel people to it, but has to be in on the talks to help to present cases, rebut assertions and provide the detailed knowledge of the production system and its workings without which no real negotiation could occur. Certainly, the trade union side will not talk until they have prepared in depth, so that the management side has to do the same.

This wide variety of challenges calls for a special breed of person. In addition to the skills needed to run the technical aspects of the production process and to manage the people, they also need to be alert to potential problems, quick to respond to them decisively, energetic to cover all of the ground, wily and resourceful, tough-minded and fit physically and mentally.

Production planning

The management of production starts from someone else's figures. Production plans cannot be made in isolation, but come about in response to customers' needs. It is usually the marketing department's sales forecast which triggers production planning.

That statement may cause hollow laughter from some production managers. In some organisations the marketing department is unable to get its sales forecast to the production people in time for them to do their detailed forecasting. An organisation with that problem has a serious institutional flaw of the kind that makes it unfit to compete.

The reason why the sales forecast does not appear in time may be due to the production department working to unrealistically long lead-times. Or it may be due to failings in the marketing department, such as:

- indolence
- withholding information for political reasons
- lack of understanding of production control issues
- inability to assemble and process information fast enough
- unavailability of essential information
- internal procedures for approval of forecasts.

Typically, unless the managers themselves are at war, marketing people will slip to production colleagues a pre-approval version of the forecast as an early, if unreliable, version of what to expect. That is helpful, and is one of the ways in which resourceful human beings strive to make organisations work despite their rules. The supreme example of the man who brought everything to a halt by following laid-down procedures was the eponymous hero of *The Good Soldier Schweik*.

Late arrival of sales forecasts can be a potent cause of war between a marketing and a production department. Production needs to know demand levels early since it will be in severe trouble if it sources too much, or has too little, raw material, creates more or less manpower capacity than is needed, or hires storage facilities that prove to be unwanted or, even worse, cancels those that it really does turn out to need. Whilst the early, unofficial version of the forecast does enable some planning to be done, its basis is dangerous since great changes in volumes and timings can come about as a result of the approval process. Even that is not as bad as the situation in an organisation where no information is passed until the (late) official forecast arrives. There the production people have to work on hunch and past experience to plan their operation and hope that, when the proper piece of paper does turn up, it bears some resemblance to their working assumptions.

A situation like that ought not to arise in the first place and certainly should not be allowed to persist. That two sets of people are forecasting independently is wasteful. Where it does happen there is something seriously wrong with the way the organisation is run.

The converse problem can arise when the marketing department is able to forecast in time and the production plan is unveiled to schedule, but the production department cannot make what has been ordered. There is some excuse in highly sensitive production processes with high failure rates, or where development is proceeding in hand with production, but none where the technology is simpler.

Again, these symptoms point to severe rot in the organisation. One manager is fond of telling the story of the men's shoe manufacturer he once worked for. Their product was in great demand, but for months at a time they remained out of stock of all sizes except 7s, which they made in abundance. The production manager could never explain convincingly when the other sizes would be made so, against all the rules, he went down to the shop floor and asked one

137

two of the staff why this should be. He got the answer in minutes. It was because the operatives could turn out most pairs of size 7, and output determined their bonuses. Nobody told them to make a balanced size-range, so they did what the system encouraged them to do (and who can blame them?). Subsequent enquiry showed that everyone's bonus, including the factory manager's, was tied to output, so that if he called for a more sensible arrangement he feared that he would cause an uproar by cutting pay. Also he would feel the effect in his own pocket. Far-fetched as it may seem, he really believed that he did not need to take action.

The sad thing about that firm was the sequel to this story. Its late and short deliveries pointed out to competitors that the market sector which it dominated was available to anyone who could run a factory sensibly. They moved in and took its business away. From having been a giant of the industry it dwindled to a point at which it was taken over by one of those very competitors who stole its market.

Once a sales forecast has been obtained by some means, legitimate or unorthodox, the production department can start its own planning. It will look at current stocks to see first if anything at all needs to be made. In the case of some products it will not, for every firm has excess stocks of one product at least at some time or another. Subtracting stocks from demand shows how much needs to be made and when.

The next step is to look at stocks of components and materials to see if they will last. If more needs to be ordered it is unlikely to be available by return, but a lead-time has to be allowed for. Certain suppliers may be unreliable, and extra stock has to be held in case they deliver late. Then the capacity of the various departments of the factory will be looked at.

It is then that the problems are exposed. The production planner knows that he needs 200 machines to be made next month, the assembly shop can put together 50 a week, but two of the components will not be available until week 3: what does he do? The usual answer is to try all the internal juggling possible and, if that fails, to lean on the supplier for at least a few items to be made early. If that does not work the marketing people have to be told either to revise their delivery date requirements or accept that promises will be broken. If they will not play, the last resort is to incur extra cost via extra shifts or casual staff from the third week onwards, or to subcontract some of the work to an outside firm. It rarely pays to pose that choice to sales staff, for their orientation towards customer service at almost any cost decides the question. Marketing people are supposed to be responsible for profit as well as sales volume, and their judgement ought therefore to be less one-sided. Ideally, they will take a balanced view of where the firm's best interest lies, whether in dropping today's profit to hold the customer or facing down the possible wrath of the customer at late delivery in order to preserve profit levels.

The production people may well hope that their marketing colleagues choose late delivery. One further reason for tension between marketing and sales is the very different set of expectations operating on each of them. This theme will be picked up later, but in this context it is important to realise that marketing people understand the need to satisfy customers, without taking it to the extremes which might be advocated by some sales people. There comes a time for many sales people at which they allow the balance between representing the organisation to the customer and representing the customer to the organisation to tip over in the wrong direction. The production people's contribution to this debate is to point out that the greatest economies come from steady, uninterrupted production of standard items.

It is often very difficult indeed for production people to accommodate alterations to plans that have been laid weeks or months in advance. If this month's forecast of sales for each of the next six months is wildly different from its predecessor, the production people may well tear their hair out. If next month's restores the cuts made this month they will tear out the marketing people's hair as well. Yet that sort of situation is far from unknown. It can easily come about through, for instance, evidence of a few major customers' interest not coming out until later than expected, and the delay being interpreted as apathy. The apportioning of blame then starts – but who is to blame in a situation like that? Optimism over their intentions would have been misplaced, and the relationships could have become strained if the salespeople had chased more strenuously. It is unfortunate, but it just has to be accepted and dealt with by the production planner.

Production management principles

The basic principle underlying production management is that a constant level of production is the easiest to manage and results in the cheapest output. Changes in the amount produced cause problems and hence expense.

Figures 17, 18 and 19 show how levels of output can vary. Steady output is the cheapest to produce, and rising and falling output the most expensive. If demand from different seasons can be overlaid (for instance, air-conditioners and heaters), it can some times produce a near-perfect overall total quantity of production.

This has already been rehearsed as a reason for friction between production and marketing people. Marketing responds to the customers' needs, and this causes demand to vary over time. The corresponding messages are passed to production, who can become deeply frustrated. Many a production manager becomes prematurely old through the effort to get marketing people to understand the realities of running a factory.

Marketing people ought to realise that constant chopping and changing of production schedules hits profits. They should also realise that large seasonal fluctuations raise costs. The marketing department should therefore pass, and keep to, two resolutions:

1. Not to change the level of production called for any more than is absolutely essential; to give plenty of warning when it has to be changed; and, when they cannot give enough warning, to explain why,

2. To develop products with a seasonal pattern which runs counter to the present one.

The first calls for a mixture of prudence and good manners. The second is common sense. If the present business peaks in the summer and falls away in the winter, products which answer winter needs ought to be developed. At the very least, techniques should be used to shift as much demand as possible out of the peak period. A major toy company which had access to cheap money from its American parent used these funds to allow dealers to take in stocks early but pay at the normal time. By carrying stocks when the trade wisdom said it was wrong, the dealers sold a lot more; and the manufacturer found that he was selling half of his output in each half of the year, said to be an impossibility in the toy trade at that time.

In some industries 24-hour, seven-day production is the norm: steelworks and other continuous process industries are obvious examples. In others, production stops at weekends and for holidays, but is continuous at other times. Coal-mining is an example. In many industries that intensity of use of assets is unknown. Some products have, by their very nature, to be made in batches, perhaps

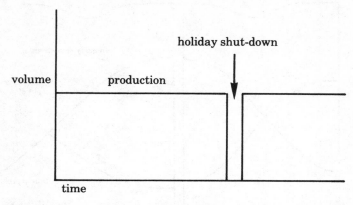

Figure 17 *The factory manager's ideal pattern of production: steady output all year long*

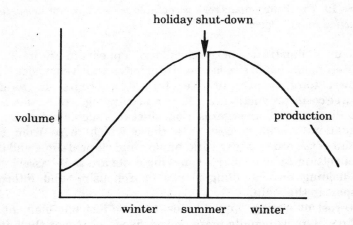

Figure 18 *The factory manager's nightmare: production rising and falling with seasonal demand*

because their raw materials are available only at certain times of the year, or because one day's production satisfies a week's needs, or for some other reason. In these cases it is important for the batch made to be neither too big nor too small. Too big, and it will incur costs of carrying the excess stock; too small and it will be less economical to make. The balancing-act between these two considerations has been considered deeply by operations analysts, for the effect on profits of getting it wrong too often can be disastrous.

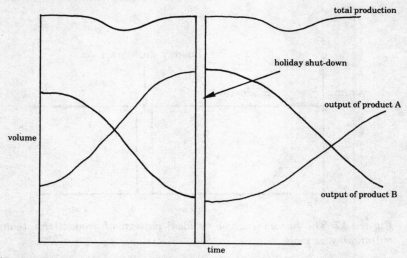

Figure 19 *The factory manager's acceptable seasonal compromise: total production roughly level*

The usual illustration of the calculation appears in Figure 20.

The economic batch size is that size of batch which coincides with the lowest total cost per unit. The total cost is, of course, the total of the three costs: production, ancillary and carrying. Production cost is usually known to an organisation, since it is such a basic item of information. Ancillary costs are those which arise from the creation of the order: paperwork, buying and clerical time, and the cost of setting up machinery. Carrying costs are those associated with holding and handling stocks: warehousing and internal transport in the main.

The cost of setting up machines, to take just one element of ancillary costs, is usually more or less fixed, whatever the batch size within normal limits. Thus it costs less per unit the larger the batch is. By contrast, the cost of carrying each item of stock usually rises as the quantity increases: a few can be tucked away in a spare corner, incurring little in the way of handling and storage cost, but a larger quantity may necessitate extra transport, rented outside warehousing and a lot more handling. That, in turn, implies further costs arising from losses and damage.

The important issue highlighted by Figure 20 is no single one of these costs but their total. The whole point of the exercise is to arrive at it. In general, the unit cost is high if either a few or a lot are made, and at its lowest somewhere between the extremes. The

142

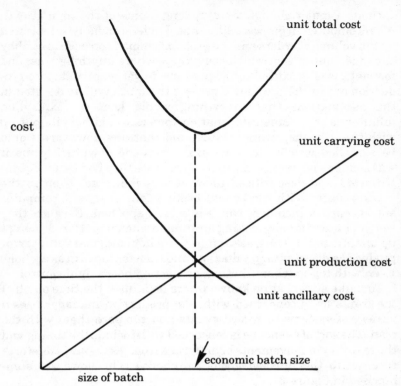

Figure 20 *Economic batch size*

point at which it is lowest dictates the ideal size of batch to make. The number actually made may be adjusted slightly to take account of practicalities: using up old raw materials, for instance, or making some extras to allow for rejects.

Managing the production process

Once the plan has been drawn up someone has to put it into practice. That part of the job may involve scrapping much of an earlier plan. To do that without a descent into chaos it is essential to know whereabouts on the previous plan one is. To change from an unknown position to one which you rapidly lose sight of is an excellent route to disaster. Incredibly, there really do exist organisations which operate on that principle, but they rarely survive

143

without a major change for very long. Some of the high-growth microcomputer firms were like that. Understandably intoxicated by the volume of orders and the great profit made on each unit, they expanded out of control. Nobody knew where anything was, and foresight was sacrificed to the pressure to get more and more production out in the present. If anyone thought at all, it resulted in the assumptions that everything would keep on expanding infinitely at the same rate, that customers would happily put up with the way they were treated, and that any downturn would be signalled well in advance. But when the downturn came it was sudden and savage, the more so because they had become so introverted and desensitised to what was really going on in the market-place. With the benefit of hindsight everyone, computer entrepreneurs included, can see what happened. Because they were not intentionally looking for trouble when it mattered, it crept up unannounced. Thus, as so often, a fundamental marketing error produced a disaster for production, and then for the firm as a whole. Even with top-notch marketing, production needs tight control.

To make sure that he knows where he is all of the time on all of the fronts he is concerned with, the production manager uses a variety of systems to record events and compare them with the plan. The sort of events he is concerned with include the timing and the quantity of movements of materials from goods-inwards stores through to the finished goods warehouse. The flows are summarised in Figure 21.

Clearly, this is a very simple summary of a very complex picture. Production managers strive constantly to ensure that it does not become confused. Many of the generalised boxes in the diagram can be broken down into further sub-sections. To illustrate that point, the rejects from the production process have been split into further divisions. They could have been broken down still more, to show the fate of rejects bought in from sub-contractors, which will almost certainly be different from those generated by the firm's unaided efforts.

It is most unlikely that anyone will have drawn up a precise plan which embraces all these systems throughout the organisation. However, there will be in the minds of people working in each section a clear picture of how their own part works and how it relates to others with which it interacts. Where no formal system exists, the people concerned will invent their own.

Individual ingenuity and initiative are not to be discouraged as a rule. As long as the home-made systems work towards the aims of

Figure 21 *Production flows summarised*

the production department they should be used. The trouble with control systems which are devised informally and locally is that they can be fine for present staff and current conditions, but incapable of adaptation to meet changed requirements and conditions. Still less can they mesh with other informal systems in parallel, upstream or downstream sections. Thus the organisation which allows its systems to grow informally is under a great threat which is completely invisible. The organisation runs smoothly and under control today, but as soon as new demands are placed upon it it is unable to deal with them. The new situation requires a quick response, so managers call for information fast. Because that question had never been anticipated, the answer simply cannot be supplied in the form which the question requires. If a manager, applying the wider vision expected of him, had designed the system rather than just letting it grow, the chances are that it would have taken into account many more factors, and thus would be better able to serve the organisation's true needs.

Group technology

Between the 1930s and the 1960s there were remarkable advances in the way in which production was organised. Much of this came about under the stimulus of emerging mass markets, and not a little was due to the pressures of a war which left few advanced nations entirely untouched. One of the most important advances was the introduction of group technology (GT).

Research had shown that the vast majority of production batches in engineering shops was for very small quantities. Yet all production areas were set up in such a way as to be ideally organised for long runs. The result was that, in some cases, as much time was being spent setting machines for a new run as was spent on the run itself. Since machines cost money whether they are working or not, this revealed a substantial area of waste. If a way could be found of reducing set-up time and improving scheduling so as to lower the number of re-sets required to deal with different runs, considerable savings would be made. GT supplied just this.

GT works by, first, classifying the factory's products into 'families' with similar characteristics. The characteristics are merged into a theoretical *composite component*, which possesses all the family's characteristics but which itself does not exist. The machines necessary to produce the composite component are then grouped together on the factory floor. Thus all the machines which produce the characteristics of the family are all in one place. Those machines are then set up to make the composite component, so that all the characteristics are available to be made. What is actually made is then determined by which processes are *left out*.

By these means startling improvements in machine productivity of 50 per cent and more were claimed, even in factories which, by general consent, were efficiently run. The benefits did not stop there: firms are known to have reduced delivery times by two-thirds and stocks by one-third.

The basic principle of GT, that of setting up the production area to make the composite component, and then by-passing certain processes to get what you want, is an interesting inversion of the conventional approach. As such it is useful well beyond the engineering world, and has been applied with success in service industries.

Work study

Work study involves systematically observing and analysing how people perform their jobs. It is most often applied to production workers because of the ease of measuring what they do, and because that is what the technique was developed for in the first place. It has a bad name for being a means of making people work unreasonably hard, but applied properly it reduces waste of materials and effort, and raises output and quality.

Work study comprises two primary branches: method study and work measurement.

Method study people use the acronym SREDIM to describe what they do:

1. Select the task which will be studied
2. Record how it is undertaken
3. Examine the facts recorded
4. Develop a better method
5. Install the new method
6. Maintain the new practice.

Work measurement is a close relative, taking the same course up to stage 3. Its fourth stage is to measure the time which the task takes. It is concerned specifically with time, so it then goes on to set out times that the new method should take. It often applies the technique of *activity sampling* – basically, noting at fixed intervals what is happening and generalising from that sample of observations. It can be surprisingly illuminating, and overcomes many of the problems associated with following people with a stopwatch.

The two techniques together are very powerful. Method study looks at how the job is done, work measurement at how long it takes. Both go into enormous detail and have a variety of approaches associated with them. The main reasons for applying work study are:

- almost certainly people are working inefficiently
- without a critical and disciplined examination no improvement is likely to come about
- The outside expert asking fundamental questions is the most powerful agent of change ever invented.

Stock control

Organisations need to control their stocks for these reasons:

- to make sure that they have enough of each item in the right place when it is needed
- to ensure that they are carrying no more stock than is necessary
- to trigger the decision to re-order at the right time
- to ensure that products to be discontinued are run down in an orderly way
- to enable reconciliation between what is known to have been bought and used with what is actually in stock.

In a nutshell, the main functions of stock control are to keep the factory running and to keep as little money and space tied up as possible.

Control is applied to all forms in which stock is held, whether as raw materials or finished goods. The basic process follows this simple pattern:

What we started the period with	100
What we got in during the period	200
Total available during the period	300
What we used during the period	250
Left over at the end of the period	50

The figure in the last line becomes the starting figure for the next period, of course. and the whole calculation can thus go on to infinity. It will be done for all items of any significance, whether expressed in terms of value or importance to the production process.

To move from recording stock movements to a system of full stock control it is necessary to add two further elements. They are time, and target levels. Recording what happened in the past is useful in a number of ways, but it does not involve looking forward. Stock control takes forecasts for the sales of products, examines present stocks and those which are on order, allows for delays between ordering and receiving the goods, and works out when orders need to be placed and how large they should be. It is then up to the purchasing department to ensure that these orders are placed and executed. There needs to be close liaison between the functions of stock control and purchasing, to ensure that changes to lead-times are communicated, to allow stock control to take account of delivery delays, and to tell purchasing when delivery promises have not been kept. In such circumstances, the production planners need to become involved. They may need to switch from making products whose components will be in short supply to those for which all the parts are available, and then to switch back when the missing items are delivered. The rule of thumb is that the shorter the warning the greater the disruption and cost involved in changing over.

The standard illustration of the stock control process is in Figure 22. When dealing with stock in general, the quantity on the warehouse floor is not necessarily the most useful piece of information to the manager. Above all he needs to know the 'free' stock figure, the amount which is left after current commitments have been met.

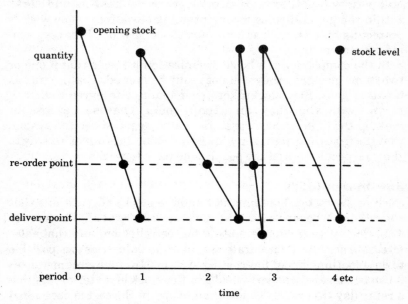

Figure 22 *Stock control chart*

Many a first-time manager has learned this the hard way. He is asked if there is enough stock to ship 1000 boxes to Thackeray's, who have just been on the telephone. He takes a quick look at the warehouse (the staff are all away at tea), sees 4000 there, and answers 'yes'. He did not know that all but 200 were about to be shipped to Dickens's, a far more important customer who ordered a month ago. Such an experience both induces stress in sales managers and proves the first-time manager's lack of vision, and is not recommended.

Stock control is also concerned with what happened to the stocks which the organisation has bought. That involves much paperwork and a close relationship with accountants. The forces have an adage: nothing moves without a piece of paper. It ought to be stuck to rigidly by all staff concerned with the stewardship and movement of stock. The stock is not their property yet it is their responsibility; if any goes missing, they cannot shrug their shoulders but must account for it. If they are unable to, suspicion of either incompetence or dishonesty or both will fall on them. Competence and honesty being essential to their remaining employed, they ensure that they can account clearly for everything in their care. It is important that the first-time manager recognises this, and works within the general rules for maintaining stock records as well as protecting his own back as far as any stock for which he is responsible is concerned.

In the complexity of a large organisation it seems that if one or two items go astray they will not really be missed. That is true, as far as it goes. Few stocktakers ever manage to agree the stock records with what they can actually count. That is no excuse for making the discrepancy worse. So many people abuse the system that the first-time manager wins friends if he goes out of his way to show respect for it and the people who have to work it.

Just-in-time (JIT)

Such is the cost of holding and handling stocks of materials that some radicals began to ask why it was necessary at all. The answer was, clearly, that suppliers could not be relied on, and that sales forecasts are often inaccurate too. In some industries it is possible to do something about forecasting systems. In some circumstances it can be more expensive to hold a buffer stock of materials against a rainy day that rarely comes than to accept the cost of occasional stock-outs. The greatest scope for improvement might lie in suppliers' performances, they thought. If early, firm orders could be given, if suppliers could be introduced to management techniques which allow late changes to production plans, and if heavy penalties could be imposed in the case of late delivery, something could be done in that area too. From these ideas was born the notion of JIT, of receiving deliveries minutes before they are needed in the factory and doing away with stocks of the most frequently used items altogether.

One of the most visible early exponents of this idea was Sainsbury's, the British supermarket chain. Tired of building new shops with large store-rooms, they decided to make over virtually all of their floor-space to selling. Thus their sales and profits improved, and with them the levels of customer service they could achieve: a wider range of goods could be offered in the extra space. It meant that, instead of taking in deliveries several times a week, deliveries had to be made to the larger stores several times a day. It demanded a sophisticated system for recording sales and stocks so as to create quick re-ordering as goods sold out of the shops. It is one element in the formula which has made Sainsbury's the supermarket with the margins the others would like to have.

The industries which are now adopting JIT tend to be in the large-scale flow-production sectors: motor vehicle assembly is an obvious example. Such is their output, any buffer stocks which they hold are big and expensive. While the technique can be imposed on suppliers only by very powerful customers, other organisations can apply its principles in order to steal a march on competitors. For example, the consumer ceramics industry in the UK has always offered its customers a delay of three months between order and delivery. One firm which took over a famous old factory has pledged to make for stock, not against orders, and is offering delivery within 48 hours of an order. Thus, by using the right supplier, even a small china shop can operate JIT to some extent, ordering on a Wednesday the stock needed for the Saturday rush.

This effect will be certain to make the interloper the supplier of first choice, and the firm whose products are the first to be promoted when a choice exists. No doubt others will follow when they find this competition hurting, and the level of service offered will be revolutionised. The wonder is that it was not done 100 years ago.

Purchasing and procurement

The function of getting the organisation's requirements bought in a disciplined way and at least cost is obviously important. In some organisations it does no more than place orders and chase for deliveries, but it ought to be more powerful than that.

The first decision which an organisation needs to take is who is permitted to place orders. Can anyone buy what he needs, or are all orders to be channelled through one person? In most organisations a little of each applies. Major items and those bought in large quantities are purchased centrally. Less significant items and some with special characteristics are bought locally. In both cases a common paperwork procedure should apply so that the order can be tied up with delivery note and invoice in due course. Under such a system there is no possibility of paying for the same item twice, or for items which were not delivered or not ordered in the first place. Those things do happen in poorly regulated organisations.

Production people have been known to question the need for a specialist buying department. Where that happens it is probably because that department is not performing the full range of functions which it ought to be, or is not communicating the fact that it is. A good buying department will:

- look at proposed suppliers in great detail and in a detached and disciplined way, and assess them ('vendor rating')
- find and use sources of supply at least total cost to the organisation (least prime cost may turn out most expensive in the long run)
- ensure that delivery does take place to time, and warn all concerned where this fails
- advise on prices, availability and delivery times
- verify invoices
- develop and enforce terms and conditions of purchase
- assist operating managers in all dealings with suppliers.

To some this list – and particularly the last item – may make it look as if the buying department is trying to extend its influence for no good reason. In fact there are all sorts of sound arguments for having the technical and specialist people's dealings with suppliers checked by a professional who has sound knowledge of the law governing the buying and selling of goods. There is many a specialist, eager to press ahead with his project, who has unwittingly established an open-ended commitment to a supplier. A supplier who is naive or unscrupulous may let that situation run until a sizeable bill has mounted up, which he has a well-documented right to collect.

Quality control

The control of quality is an area carrying huge implications for internal costs and external relations. If customers are to be happy with the product it must perform to the specification agreed or assumed, for at least as long as is acceptable. Quality control (QC) is therefore concerned with two related issues: quality (the extent to which the product is fit for its purpose) and reliability (the extent of its ability to continue to work to the quality standard).

Thus the word 'quality' has a special and specific meaning in industry. In everyday speech, high quality is more or less undefinable and is loosely associated with luxury goods. The term is used here in its special, industrial sense.

Quality breaks down into two further divisions: quality of design (the extent to which the design itself achieves the purpose) and quality of conformance (the closeness with which the output resembles the design).

Raising quality costs money by increasing internal costs. It may also save money, by lowering the tangible and intangible cost of dealing with customers. It can also make money, by (for instance) gaining for the product a reputation which creates extra sales. The lowest quality is cheapest to make, but fetches a low price and attracts many complaints, so it is rarely profitable. The highest quality achievable costs a vast amount to accomplish, but customers might be reluctant to pay for it so it, too, is not profitable. Somewhere between the two lies a point where a little less quality fetches a rather lower price, and a little more quality fetches only a slightly higher price. In other words, the return on the investment in quality is at its highest.

QC does not aim to eliminate customer complaints, but to control them down to a predetermined level at which supplier and customer can stand the damage. The idea of what limits are acceptable varies from product to product. If a lettuce is less crisp than he expects, the customer shrugs his shoulders and resolves to choose more carefully next time. If a turbine blade from a jet engine lacks the right degree of crispness it could cause the deaths of hundreds of people. Even so, the jet engine manufacturers know that they can never eliminate error; they dedicate themselves to holding it down to a stupendously low level.

The extent of the precautions taken do sound as if they are aimed at error elimination, but these engineers are not arrogant and they are realists. The manufacturer keeps records of the sources of every one of the thousands of components used in each engine. The suppliers keep similar records, all the way back to the steel mill which made the material from which the turbine blade was created. This means that if a fault is discovered in one component in one of the four engines in a Jumbo in Singapore, all the aircraft from around the world with engines containing components from the same batch can be grounded immediately for investigation. Many lives have been saved by this system, which justifies its great cost.

Unfortunately, the world is full of organisations which maintain standards of quality which are far higher than is appropriate. This is not an argument for shoddy goods (see page 153) but a plea for the reduction of waste and thus of cost. Unnecessary over-specification costs everyone money and depletes scarce resources wastefully.

Excess quality often stems from engineers' and production people's professional pride. The same can apply to innovations in products, which may be quite unnecessary from a marketing point of view, and can even add to unreliability. It is a fact that reliability stems from the use of simple designs with least components and proven manufacturing methods. Components which are likely to fail can be double or treble banked, and the design can see to it that failure leads to safety (the vehicle's throttle drops to tickover when the cable snaps, rather than flying up to full power).

Testing is important in establishing reliability. What is usually found is that failures are relatively common in the early and late stages of a product's life. At the beginning the failures due to faulty assembly or substandard components show up; at the end it is wearing out. Early failure is infuriating to the customer and embarrassing to the supplier, so that many firms run in their products before delivery. Then most of the early failures occur before delivery and red faces are saved all round.

Many firms who are in a powerful position in relation to suppliers buy on the basis that goods will be accepted only if a certain proportion of a sample taken from each delivery passes a quality test. If too many of that sample are faulty, the entire consignment is returned. Such a deal sharpens suppliers' attitudes wonderfully.

Mention of sampling reintroduces the topic of statistics. They are the basis of the quality controller's basic tool, the QC Chart, shown in Figure 23. This is a more detailed version of the one which appeared in general form in Figure 7. The samples are taken strictly of the predetermined number and at exactly the correct times. They are measured, and their mean plotted on the chart. If the reading strays into a warning area, further samples are taken to check on the first sample's reliability. If it moves into the action area, the machine is stopped and reset.

Levels for action and warning are calculated statistically (by

Figure 23 *Quality control chart in detail*

standard errors, for anyone who is interested). This application of statistical techniques is extremely useful in cutting the cost of inspection within a predetermined level of risk that the sample taken might not be representative.

Value analysis

Value analysis is a close relation of QC. QC concerns itself with the design's achievement of its purpose and the closeness of the finished product to its design. VA looks at function, that is to say at the 'purpose' to which QC relates.

VA does not start by looking at what is being done now. Its interest is in the function which the product is intended to perform, in order to see if that function can be performed more cost-effectively than by the present method. Usually a product performs more than one function, but there is generally a single purpose which stands out clearly as the main reason for its existence. Attention is paid to that in the first place. A very precise statement of function is made, pared down to the minimum. Far from being an exercise in pedantry it is meant to result in the clearest and most economical statement of what the product is for.

From that statement the value analyst proceeds to look at other ways in which the same function could be achieved, in the hope that one will come up which is more cost-effective.

155

It is worth spending a moment to consider what is meant by the term value. Value is a concept which can be thought of in three ways:

Exchange value: what a buyer will pay for a product

Use value: what the buyer will pay for the practical function which the product carries out

Esteem value: the extra which the buyer will pay over and above the use value.

It is readily seen that the first is the total of the other two. The way in which they combine can vary dramatically. Consider two cars, one a Mercedes the other a Ford. The use value of each is more or less identical, but the esteem value of one is far higher than that of the other. Thus the exchange values are markedly different. The same exercise can be conducted in every field in which products and services are bought and sold.

The clever manufacturer is trying all the time to add esteem value to his products. Many manage to do so, usually by marketing methods, and the difference in price that can be achieved has transformed many a company's fortunes.

So far it may have sounded as if the value analyst is merely a theorist. Not so. His most frequent contribution comes via design improvements within products which he stimulates by asking of each internal function:

- Does this have to be done at all?
- If so, must it be done this way?
- Is there a better way?

Rarely is VA a solo performance. It can be started by one person but it requires the involvement of people from production, marketing, accounting and design departments, and sometimes even outside suppliers.

Variety reduction

A good way of increasing costs is to make a wider variety of components or finished products than is actually necessary. Some sales departments and the weaker marketing department will encourage their production colleagues to make virtually a different product for each customer. Every change in production incurs cost, and changes should therefore be kept to a minimum.

The problem is that any range of products has a tendency to grow in number. Therefore determination is needed to restrict growth to what is demonstrably desirable. As with finished products so with their components. Common components should be used as much as possible to create the variations in output.

One of the best examples of that last point is a leading car manufacturer. In Europe it offers over 100 varieties of cars from fewer than a dozen bodyshells and engine blocks.

Premises location

The choice of where the office, laboratory, warehouse or factory should be put is made in the light of a large number of factors, uniquely combined for each industry, each organisation within it and each location within an organisation.

Usually the first consideration is whether or not to expand the existing facility. In the UK that option scarcely existed for many firms until the 1980s. Successive governments had agreed that the prosperous south-east should not enjoy further growth, and that expansions of any scale at all should be forbidden, unless they were undertaken in the more needy parts of the country. That led, over the years, to the building of many factories in odd locations, few of which survived the closures of the early 1980s. In the public sector, the government established a special unit to push civil service jobs out of London.

Those days are gone, and a freer market now exists. Thus decisions can be taken more in line with what an organisation perceives its interests to be. Labour is certainly a crucial determinant for many organisations. Raw numbers of unemployed are not enough, otherwise organisations would be flocking to the worst blackspots. Skills and the capacity to learn, with a supporting educational infrastructure, are recognised increasingly as being of prime importance.

In many quarters grants are thought to play a large part in relocation decisions, but studies suggest that they go mainly to organisations which would have opened in that location anyway. Their effectiveness is perhaps diluted by the suspicion of some managers that grants are offered only to move them to undesirable locations, in which they will be stuck for ever in return for a one-off gift.

Clearly an organisation must investigate factors other than grants. Among them are housing, schools and the general environment. If these are not attractive to key staff the chances are that

157

they will decline to move, wrecking – or at least severely damaging – the entire exercise. From the point of view of the organisation's operations, it needs to know about the passenger and freight transport service, suppliers, sites with the right characteristics, and the attitude of the local authority regime. In special cases there might be political and safety considerations, not to mention accessibility to the MD's home, and whether this location fits in with the organisation's other sites and its markets.

Usually one of the most influential factors which is most influential is the cost of getting materials in, and finished goods out to customers. Unlike so many of the other factors it lends itself to numerical analysis. There are some very clever computer programs which will guide a firm to pick the best location for its operations. Nevertheless, some odd factors do come into play sometimes. One American, briefed to set up a UK subsidiary, looked at the rainfall map to determine his general area of search, then identified the good rail and road links within the area of least precipitation, cut them off at a distance of 70 miles from London, and picked three towns to look at. A similarly scientific method was used to locate its production, not near its offices, but first in south Wales and then in the north-east of England. To cap it all, a later MD moved the HQ by 80 miles. Then they moved that to the north east too. Doubtless all kinds of numerical analysis were done in each case to justify decisions already half-taken. If it was, the information was used as a drunk uses a lamp-post: for support rather than illumination.

Factory design and layout

The last thing anyone designing a new factory should do is to think what it ought to look like from the outside. The floor layout should be designed first, and in meticulous detail. Only when everyone is quite sure that the layout will work should any thought be given to putting walls and a roof over it. That is a slight exaggeration, for people will enquire about economical roofing spans before designing layouts which can be built over only at prodigious cost. It is also a statement of an ideal for most organisations, since they have somehow to fit their operations into an existing building. Here compromises will be needed, but there is usually more than one building to choose from. The trick is to choose the building which enforces fewest compromises on unimportant matters. Once the building has been chosen you are more or less stuck with it, so it is important to get as close to the ideal as possible. Indeed, when organisations are putting up buildings for their own particular needs they often create something which is over-specified. That is because they have an eye to the future. The commissioning organisation may place only light loadings on floors, but does not specify that the building should meet just their own needs. They build to more exacting standards because if their policy, products or processes change they do not want to undertake costly and inconvenient alterations. If the worst happens and they need to sell the building quickly, a general-purpose building should be more in demand than one with only a specialised application.

It is easy to underestimate the space which will be required by not allowing enough for unused space. The gaps between machines may look great, but when work-in-progress and materials are being moved around they can prove inadequate. Increased height in a building raises not only the construction cost, but also that of keeping the building lit and heated. The relation between these matters and safety is obvious, but there are other effects which justify the use of special advisers. For example, a lighting tube flashes imperceptibly at a speed so fast that it looks like a steady source of light. If it does so at the same speed as a piece of machinery rotates, it can set up a stroboscopic effect which makes the machine appear to be stationary. Someone puts his hand on the moving part, and there is a horrible accident.

The availability of services within the building also deserves foresight. Requirements will change, and provision made today for future access to electricity, water, gas, telephone and data circuits and so forth will be far cheaper and more convenient than breaking into them afresh at some later date. That point – forethought and provision for the future – applies to every aspect of the building's design. Otherwise the fixed requrements for waste disposal, vehicle turning areas and access points may be so inflexible and costly to change as to scupper future plans for development.

Within the building the layout is the single most important consideration. Poor layout leads to extra handling, and even to complete confusion. The first rule is to have a one-way system. Production may start at one end of the building, flow straight on and eventually emerge from the other end, having turned neither left nor right. Or it might start in one corner, run all round the building in a curve, and out at the preceding corner. It could also mix these approaches, but as long as it flows in one direction only it follows the first principle.

The second principle is that the route should be as short as possible. The least distance between machines (as long as it is safe), and the less handling, the better. In this context it ought to be remembered that the factory exists in three dimensions: it has air space which can be used as well as floor area. Indeed, many a consultant has found that he can save a client the cost of an expensive extension by making better use of the height of the existing building.

Next the question of flexibility is considered in relation to future changes. Clearly, equipment should not be sited so close to walls that it cannot be maintained properly, or so as to obscure service points, safety exits and so on. Hidey-holes have a habit of appearing in any factory as if from thin air, and they should be strongly discouraged: all operations should be clearly visible. That stricture covers those officially sanctioned refuges such as special enclosures, shop-floor offices and stores. They limit flexibility and reduce the amount of floor-space available for use. Moreover, they can start an unwholesome status race between departments to outbid each other in the size and solidity of these possessions. They do not apply where it is absolutely necessary, such as where security or accommodation has to be provided, but great care should be exercised in the placing of fixed obstructions.

Safety of people is very important, and comfort is closely related to it. To aid it, gangways should be wide enough for emergency equipment to pass, and clearly painted on the floor. They should never be obstructed. Rules about smoking should be explicit and understood by all: many organisations allocate a special area to which smokers must go before lighting up. That is not a means of oppression, but a sensible precaution against a known fire risk and a way of protecting the health of others. Advice on safety matters in general is freely available from the officials of the Health and Safety Executive and fire and building regulations departments. Like most officials, they would prefer to get the problems ironed out at the planning stage, rather than having to take enforcement action against a dangerous installation.

Make or buy?

Often a management is faced with having to decide whether to buy in parts and components for their range of products – or even a complete piece of equipment – or make their own. The criteria are usually:

- the degree to which current capacity is utilised
- relative costs
- strategic importance to the organisation
- quality performance of vendors versus own production
- vendor reliability.

If the factory is half-empty and the product is one which it could make, the decision almost makes itself. That would probably apply even where the made-in cost was higher than the bought-in price, because the internal cost will include an element for overheads which will otherwise go unrecovered.

Sub-contractors can be unreliable in delivery times and in quality. Many a firm was set up on the assumption that it would buy in made parts and confine itself to assembly, but was forced by suppliers' poor performance to make the parts itself. Even where the policy is to buy in, a firm will sometimes make a part of its requirements itself for strategic reasons. If lack of the part could halt production altogether it is quite usual to source it from more than one supplier, including in-house manufacture, so that a fire, strike or other mishap at one will not close down the organisation's entire production

Research and development, and new products

Production people are always influenced by R&D matters, and are sometimes responsible for them. R&D covers a number of basic functions, the main ones being the improvement of existing products and methods and the development of new. R&D is therefore rarely conducted in a vacuum, but involves input from departments responsible for production, marketing and also accounting and others. Marketing have to be happy that changed specifications will at least not harm customers' and users' interests. Accountants and work-study people want to ensure that any expected savings will not be illusory. Buyers will advise on availability and get quotations for any new parts and materials. Employees will need to be told about the change and why it is necessary, and trainers will have to ensure that people understand any new methods. In some situations the law could even be involved, if methods or materials are hazardous. Insurers and patent experts may be consulted, new maintenance schedules created, and many more people required to contribute. The list of people to be involved must not be skimped in some attempt to save them time and trouble. To do so merely postpones any problems, which is a sure way of amplifying them.

The reasons for R&D projects can be very diverse. They can stem from desperation at falling sales of existing products, from caution which dictates the spreading of risk, from ambition to beat competitors and many more reasons – including the desire to exploit the unexpected opportunity which luckily presents itself.

A vital matter which is sometimes overlooked is that industrial R&D has to be for clearly defined and understood projects. Research into only broadly defined areas, in the hope that something useful will turn up is a category for the few with either deep pockets or no need to show a tangible return on their expenditure. For that reason it is usually confined to the academic world, specialised research institutions and the very largest international corporations.

One area which industry often overlooks is the output of the academic research world. Theses, papers and research reports are pouring out in a vast and growing stream. In the academic culture, information is for publishing almost irrespective of its commercial worth, although that altruism is coming under increasing pressure as funding fails to grow at the rate of spending. Anyone in the organisational world will find it worthwhile to search the literature for work related to his own field of interest. It can be painstaking and plodding work, but the help of an academic librarian cuts it down appreciably. Not only can it yield information of immediate usefulness, but following up a lead brings the manager into personal contact with people working in his field. They are invariably great enthusiasts for it, and will talk freely to anyone who shows an interest. Indeed, so great can their contribution be that some organisations decide not to undertake their own research work but to contract it out.

Whatever the way in which R&D is organised it is vital that it serves the needs of both production and marketing departments: marketing for new products and improvements, production for better methods and materials.

Maintenance

Plant and buildings have to be maintained or their useful lives are considerably shortened. Moreover, they may become dangerous if neglected.

Maintenance takes two forms: routine maintenance for protective reasons and the emergency repair after a failure. The former is planned for and undertaken in an orderly way to fit in with times when machines are normally idle. The latter is, by definition, unexpected. Nevertheless provision has to be made for it.

As with other production matters, cost is an important aspect. It is foolish to look at the cost of maintenance in isolation. Rather, the whole-life cost of equipment should be considered, which includes the cost of maintenance as well as that of purchase. Once it has been decided which machine to buy, the cost of maintenance to the necessary standard is merely a consequence of that decision and not an independent issue.

To be sure that maintenance is being conducted to schedule each piece of equipment should have a log in which all maintenance, breakdowns and usage is recorded. Logs should be inspected regularly by the manager responsible, who should also carry out spot checks to see that what is said to have been done has actually been done.

Where sudden failure occurs the production department has to decide whether or not to halt production completely, or whether the unserviceable machine can simply be by-passed while the shift is completed. As soon as it is available to them, the maintenance team descends on it and keeps on working until it is put right. The cost of paying them to work round the clock may be high, but it is usually a lot less than keeping an entire factory or department idle during working hours. For that reason the contracts of employment of maintenance people usually require flexible working. Some firms do not keep their own maintenance team, or restrict it to particular activities. They use outside specialists to make repairs, often from their equipment suppliers. Whether or not that is more economical over a year than keeping an in-house team is usually decided by the number of breakdowns, the length of time each repair takes, the cost of idle time, and the repair gang's response-time, cost and general reliability.

Trade unions

Day-to-day contact with trade unions is most prevalent in those departments responsible for providing what the organisation sells which, for simplicity, are referred to here as the production departments. The first line of contact is with shop stewards (whose title varies in some industries), the representatives chosen from among their own number by the workers on the shop floor. From time to time the full-time officers, employees of the union itself, may be called in; that is usually when some major issue crops up. Such circumstances would include a major accident, a disputed dismissal, a threatened walk-out, or the annual round of pay bargaining.

Contrary to the popular view, most shop stewards are not lunatic revolutionaries who believe that disrupting the organisation which employs them will bring about a communist government. The vast majority are people with a sense of fair play and concern to see justice prevail. Managers fortunate to have shop stewards like that should give them every support they can, not because they are bosses' puppets but because they have the true interests of the organisation at heart.

There remains the small proportion of difficult individuals. Most people will not vote for folk like them except in very special circumstances: when they see them as their best champion against a difficult management. If you are being treated badly by a bunch of swine you do not pick a mild-mannered, reasonable man to fight for you but the nastiest bit of work you can find. Thus managements tend to get the unions they deserve. If management is fulfilling its true calling properly there is, in theory, no need for a union to defend the interests of staff against those of the organisation. Nevertheless, many enlightened managements encourage union membership so as to have a conduit for the feelings and preoccupations of employees.

Foremen and supervisors

Supervisors and foremen and women have a difficult job in most organisations. Typically they are recruited to that position after proving themselves the most conscientious and effective of the shop-floor people. They are made responsible for the performance of the whole section, including that of people who do not share their values. Then they are left on their own to get on with running things, the assumption being that doing the job well proves you can supervise others doing it. It is a huge leap, from responsibility solely for one's own output to that for other people's. It involves learning new skills, mainly in the field of managing people, and acquiring new knowledge of what one is allowed to offer by way of sticks and carrots.

These are serious issues, for all over the world there are supervisors in organisations large and small, public and private, in manufacturing and service industries, who are taken from the shop floor and expected to make themselves into managers. It is probably easier to convert an accountant into an MD than to make an operative into a supervisor. For the supervisor is undoubtedly a manager, responsible for the work of others and required to get results. Yet if he has never been trained in the elements of management, what chance does he have? The untrained manager too often goes to one of two extremes: he capitulates to the pressure on him from below, or he becomes a martinet. Either way, his people will sense that all is not well and will start to develop a sense of failure. The supervisor feels isolated. He does not dare to confide in his boss, for fear of being thought incompetent, and his former workmates shun him as a 'boss's man'. Organisations owe it to themselves and to their supervisors to select the right people for that demanding role in the first place, and then to train them to be as effective as both sides would wish them to be.

Training is at the heart of supervisory effectiveness, and effective supervisors are the key to sound shop-floor operations. If good supervisors are placed in an organisational context that makes sense, production can flourish.

The law

The law affects the production department in many ways. The two areas of greatest concern to the operating manager are to do with health and safety and with the protection of employees' rights. Thus emphasis is often placed on production people understanding their duty to work in a safe manner, and on production managers – supervisors included – realising that defined procedures have to be followed if people misbehave; they cannot just be fired at will.

Where it is involved with buying, the production department is concerned with the law of contract. The same body of law affects what it provides for the customers to buy. In addition, if it behaves in an actionably negligent way the production department places at risk the funds and reputation of the entire organisation.

Some people regard the law as a nuisance which limits their right to behave as they wish. That attitude contains the seeds of the very cause of the law's intervention in the first place. The first Factory Acts were brought about solely by the sense of outrage felt by decent people at the behaviour of Victorian manufacturers. The latter defended their actions in a number of ways, including the argument that, if people did not like the conditions, they could go elsewhere. In other words, the factory owner had a perfect right to behave abominably and it was up to the staff to vote with their feet if they objected. More recently, controls on polluting effluents have been introduced for one reason only: that manufacturers thought that they had a perfect right to dump their muck on other people's doorsteps. Thus, if the organisation does not want the law to interfere with its operations it ought to make sure that it is not behaving offensively. Because they fear that legislation could prove inflexible and unpleasant to contend with, many industries have set up self-policing arrangements. These generally comprise a voluntary code of conduct and a disciplinary system for dealing with offenders. Where they are effective, most people within and outside the industry would agree that they are preferable to getting Parliament involved. Nevertheless, the lawmakers must never lose sight of the fact that it is the threat of legislation that keeps these arrangements effective.

Chapter 7
Finance and Accounting

To many outsiders the art and science of accountancy is a closed book. Two factors may be responsible for most of this effect: the increasing complexity of the legal requirements for disclosure and taxation, and the great skill with which the accountancy profession has limited entry to its ranks. This has been done in part by progressively raising the educational requirements for acceptance into articled clerkship (apprenticeship to the rest of us), which may be no bad thing. There are two obvious consequences of the resulting shortage of fully trained accountants: salaries are ever increasing, and more and more people are training via less conventional methods.

Along with the rise in demand for accountants membership of the leading institutes is growing. The three main ones are the Institute of Chartered Accountants, the most prestige-laden body of them all, the Chartered Institute of Public Finance and Accountancy, which specialises in issues of public sector accounting, and the Chartered Institute of Management Accountants. Management accounting, or cost accounting as it used to be called before it extended its influence beyond the costing arena, deals with the day-to-day task of keeping the organisation going, part of which involves forecasting. Together with the company secretary (served by the Chartered Institute of Secretaries) they cover the whole spectrum of the organisation's financial and legal concerns.

What accountants are for

The primary attitudes and skills which a chartered accountant brings to an organisation are:

- an understanding of finance: where money comes from, at what price and on what terms
- an understanding of systems for financial control
- knowledge of how the law relating to accounting and taxation must be applied
- prudence, clear-mindedness and a grasp of the totality as well as the detail of systems.

The first three items on that list are predictable, but the last is no less important. Indeed, it reflects the greatest contribution which accountants can make to organisational decisions. To the hard-driving sales manager or the energetic production man looking for big savings, the accountant can look like a real nuisance. He seems to lack vision, and can only pick holes in what the other wants to do. The annoying thing is that his considered criticisms are usually perfectly accurate. They need to be, for often they are the only thing standing between survival and organisational suicide. Of course there are accountants who are over-cautious and so concerned with minutiae that they cannot see the big picture, just as there are airline pilots, jockeys, musicians and surgeons with the same characteristics. However, a manager usually comes unstuck when he ignores an accountant's advice.

The first-time manager in particular can learn a great deal at the knee of an accountant. When he encounters one he should take the chance to find out how the accountant views his function. If he is prepared to listen, and the accountant to talk, he will rapidly see how the influence of the accounting department reaches through the entire organisation from top to bottom and from side to side.

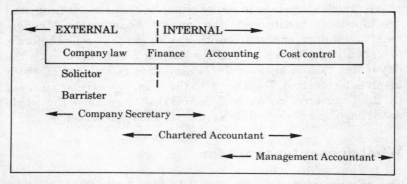

Figure 24 *The spans of professionals' authority within a private-sector organisation*

That pervasiveness helps to explain why accountants so often become chief executives. Theirs is the only department in an organisation whose trade is the understanding in financial terms of what all the others are up to, and the medium in which they work – money – is that in which efficiency and effectiveness are most often measured.

A company accountant will say that his job covers several broad responsibilities and activities. As with other departments they involve internal, departmental responsibilities as well as interactions with the wider world:

The accounting department
Invoicing and credit control
Paying debts
Maintaining statutory records
Negotiating with tax-collecting bodies
Organising and facilitating audits

For other departments
Facilitating the setting of targets
Advising on and operating costing systems
Capital investment appraisal

For the organisation at large
Recording individual and overall performance
Aggregating individual targets and performances to agree
    with overall aims and performance
Forecasting the financial position
Producing statutory accounts
Designing, installing and maintaining systems to enable
    all this to happen on time.

In addition, if the accountant has responsibility for sourcing finance, he will also represent the organisation to banks and other financial institutions, and support the finance director and chairman in their representations to City analysts and journalists.

It is most important that the accounting department has at least great influence over – and preferably total control of – the systems used by operating managers to conduct forward planning and to assess their future financial performance. The main reason for this is obvious: the organisation cannot be run on a series of unrelated and incompatible home-made systems. The systems used by each department must be welded into an organisation-wide whole. Furthermore, amateur systems do not always take into account all the factors which a professional recognises, and they are therefore usually inaccurate, sometimes dangerously so.

This point highlights one of the accountant's prime effects on an organisation. It is to introduce and maintain a consistency of approach to financial matters. So strong is belief in the value of consistency in the way results are calculated and reported that investors look with great suspicion on firms which change the basis for accounting in their annual reports. They may argue that they are trying to reflect reality more closely, but the hard-bitten investor knows from experience that such changes are too often made to cover up a mediocre performance. Any financial director will resist proposals to change accounting conventions needlessly, and it will take very strong arguments to convince him of a need. So the first-time manager who rails against the unfairness of the reporting system in reflecting his results will usually do so in vain. His best course of action may be to do one of two things: to keep and publish parallel records on a more realistic basis, or to give the organisation results which show up as good on the reports. The first approach may be laborious, the second cynical or realistic, depending on your point of view.

The accountant's obsession with consistency is not pedantic. It comes from a commitment to the idea that figures for the current period ought to be capable of direct comparison with those from any other period in the organisation's existence (inflation makes that difficult enough, but the accountant would argue that this is no reason to make it completely impossible). That, in turn, springs from the allegiances which the accountant has. His first loyalty is to professional standards, and his second to his employer. If asked by his employer to compromise on what he knows to be right he would rather resign than comply. It is upon that structure of allegiances that the credibility of the figures he produces rests. A company in trouble might prefer to conceal rather than disclose its difficulties, but the fact that this is not easy to do is what creates confidence on the part of shareholders and lenders.

This issue surfaces during audits. By law every limited company has to have its annual accounts audited by an outside firm of professional accountants. Fascinating clashes of interest can occur when the auditing arm of the accountancy firm questions the propriety of actions undertaken at the instigation of its colleagues in another branch. In order to minimise this, the auditors are usually consulted over any proposed changes before they are implemented. If they draw the line, the proposal is usually killed. Unwise directors try to pressure the auditors to look leniently on their creative accounting, but such attempts are very misguided. If the initial rebuff is not enough to bring the effort to an end, the auditors may feel that they have to resign. Among investors that is seen as a most damaging event. Appointing a different firm because it has quoted a lower figure is one thing, but losing the auditors by inviting them to behave improperly is quite another.

While on the subject of audits, there is a common misunderstanding about their purpose. They are not designed to uncover all possible misdemeanours: that is the task of the Fraud Squad, not an auditor. Auditors are watchdogs who check by sampling that correct conventions are being applied and proper records are being kept.

The accountant worships at four altars:

- accuracy
- clarity
- timeliness
- consistency.

His colleagues from other disciplines, often with vastly different training and commercial experience, frequently fill him with despair. Their muddled thinking, lack of numeracy, sloppiness in administration – all are sources of frustration. That can lead to the accountant seeing himself as the only person fit to manage, and to take upon himself the job of forcing them to run their departments properly. Where it does, the others can be put on the defensive. The fact that the accountant supports his statements with specific figures can be very intimidating when the only response is a statement of conviction. That can help him to win arguments. The aggressive accountant who gets the bit between his teeth can have all his colleagues on the run.

Exciting though the sight of his colleagues in flight may be to that sort of person, this form of behaviour is not necessarily best for the organisation as a whole. Many of the best business decisions are based on judgement which, by definition, cannot be expressed in precise figures: the closest that numbers can come is an expression of probability. But mathematical calculations of probability are not what caused the judgement to be made. Judgement is more elusive than that.

The colleagues of such an accountant may be able to redress the balance by learning some of his skills. If they understand the basis of the main accounting concepts they can argue back at his figures, challenge his method of calculation and, most powerful of all, point out the deficiencies of all the accounting methods which could be brought to bear on the point at issue. There is plenty of evidence for challenging the way in which accountants do their sums, for they are a very self-critical body of people. Their professional press and their academic branch rage with controversy over virtually everything they do. There is one great truth which no honest accountant will try to conceal: *important areas of accounting are largely expressions of opinion, and it can be misleading to offer exact figures without a full statement of the assumption which produced them.*

Unfortunately, all that most people ever see is the bare figures. A few points to explain the problem appear in Figure 25. They are meant to give a general indication, rather than an exhaustive discussion of one aspect of the issue.

Accountants are perfectly familiar with these points, of course. They have no real alternative to taking refuge in the fact that everyone else is reporting results on the same questionable basis, so that any individual set of figures is as good (or bad) as those of the herd. It does not stop the thinkers of the profession from being deeply concerned about the misrepresentation involved and from trying to evolve methods which show more accurately what is going on.

One area in which they have achieved a success in recent years is that of accounting for inflation. In the rapid inflation of the 1970s any firm which held stocks found that its reported profits gained artificially from the falling value of money. Anti-capitalists got grim satisfaction from seeing them paying tax on those imaginary extra profits (a position which the government of the day moved rapidly to alter). After lengthy debate and much controversy the profession decided that, yes, it did want to show results in a form which eliminated the effect of inflation but no, it was too complex to apply to every aspect of reporting. So they continued to report in current money, mixing yesterday's pounds with today's quite indiscriminately, but the larger firms now include a page in their annual reports showing what effect adjustments for inflation would have. It is far from perfect but it is a response to a real problem.

Here we are touching on the accountants' Achilles' heel. The two great points of weakness of our system of accounting are:

- everything is expressed in terms of money
- reports look at the organisation solely as a going concern.

To be able to measure an organisation's achievements in terms of

172

COMPANY PROFITS AND DEPRECIATION

A company's profits are calculated by subtracting costs from the value of sales. But what are 'costs'? Accountancy convention treats depreciation as a cost. It therefore solemnly writes down the value of freehold factories and each year subtracts an amount from profits to allow for their depreciation. Yet in many areas they have trebled in value in a decade or so. Only when a revaluation of property is undertaken is the nonsense corrected, but that is done infrequently and has a disproportionate effect on the profit reported for the year in which it is done. On the one hand, firms are reluctant to revalue since the City will expect them to produce a higher return on the higher value of assets which it discloses; and on the other hand they are eager to, since the take-over sharks are forever seeking firms with undervalued assets.

To take another example, motor vehicles are written down quite rapidly, often at 25 per cent a year. Everyone is familiar with the case of the chairman's Rolls-Royce which maintains its value in money terms, and of the little-used office manager's car which is sold for a lot more than its value on the books. The over-allowance for depreciation is revealed when they are sold, but meantime profits have been understated. Some will say that the way in which the fleet of vehicles is pooled for depreciation calculations offsets the effect of a minority of vehicles which are over or under depreciated. That may be so, but where is our precision now?

Thus the idea of depreciation, like so many other accounting ideas, is thrown by changes in the value of money in relation to assets, and by movements in the value of assets relative to one another. This important cost, like so many others, turns out on examination to be based more on opinion and convention than any objective valuation. If costs are opinions, profit has to be an opinion itself.

Figure 25 *Company profits and opinion*

money is important. To do it solely in those terms is ludicrous, and about as sensible as judging the worth of a person by his income alone. It would be even sillier to report only those achievements which lend themselves to money measurement. Yet those nonsenses are at the heart of the conventions of accounting. Perhaps that is not the fault of accountancy as such, but more a default on the part of those who ought to lay emphasis on other aspects as well.

An organisation might be training its people to levels of competitiveness well above those of its domestic counterparts. That would be an expensive and necessary prelude to domination of home and overseas markets. Yet the accountants will report that the training expenditure has made it less profitable, with no way of recording the gain to the firm's ability. If the same money had been spent on a fancy but unproductive office block, flashy furniture and new cars all round, the accounts would have recorded the gain to the firm's wealth in great detail.

Likewise, the assumption that the firm is a going concern produces some questionable reports. Firms do fail, unfortunately. Such a firm's assets may be written down to nothing by depreciation, but be worth huge sums on the nostalgia market. The delivery truck bought in 1921 and laid up since 1939 is valued at nothing in the accounts, yet is worth tens of thousands of pounds.

The purpose of these words must not be misunderstood. They are not an attack on accountants or accountancy, but a plea to non-accountants to put in the work necessary to understand the conventions which their accounting colleagues use. A degree of understanding is vital, for accountancy views should not be allowed to dominate decision-making. By understanding something of the conventions the first-time manager equips himself in three important ways:

- to understand the accounts and accountants better
- to see the strengths of the accountancy approach
- to see the shortcomings and failings of the accountancy approach, and thus to question their validity in any given situation.

If a first-time manager is in an accounting function he will do well to read carefully chapters other than this one. The content of this chapter and more will be covered in his professional training. Accountants can unwittingly cause more trouble and be of least help when they overlook the fact that so many of the most important

important areas of organisational life are not susceptible to numerical treatment.

The accountant and the financial world

The ideal of every organisation would be to keep going by means of funds it generates from its own operations. Very few private sector organisations with any ambition to grow can achieve that position, and in the public sector they tend to absorb rather than create funds.

In the private sector finance comes in two forms, equity and loan. Equity is part of the permanent funds of the organisation, and is raised by the sale of shares and the retention of profits. In return for their money, shareholders expect some degree of control to be given up by the management. In the case of ordinary shares, it introduces new shareholders who may or may not agree with the directors' ideas of how the organisation ought to be run. If enough of them feel sufficiently aggrieved, they can dismiss the board of directors. Ordinary shareholders are the real risk-takers, who get a share of any profits but are the last to be paid out if the firm fails. They get their benefit in two ways: dividends (share of profits) and capital appreciation. The latter takes place usually as a result of the firm's earnings rising so that other investors can see that the shares are worth paying more for.

There are also non-voting types of equity investment, such as Preference shares, which carry a rate of interest instead of a share of any profits; it has to be paid whether or not the profit is there to support it. The 'preference' in their name arises from the fact that they are paid out before ordinary shareholders in the case of failure.

Loans are not free from obligation. Usually they will be secured on both some tangible asset and on the stock and the cash coming in as invoices are paid. Thus, whatever form finance from outside the firm takes, it is usually accompanied by a loss of control.

Loss of control means that top managers have to keep the financiers happy or risk being replaced. The financier is looking first for security, that is, not to lose his money. Once he is assured on that point he looks for a return. The form which that return takes varies with the investor. Some make their money by buying and selling quickly, others by relying on income and capital growth from a more or less stable portfolio of carefully chosen stocks. The first type wants flashy performance now, so that his shares will rise

175

a few pence and enable him to take his profit fast. The second is more likely to be sympathetic to ploughing-in of revenue to produce long-term growth, for example via training programmes.

All this places great pressure on company chairmen to run round the City explaining what the firm is doing and why. That work results in a lot of the press stories about company performance which read as if they come about through divine revelation. If it keeps the share price up it makes the firm difficult for a predator to afford, and makes it cheaper for the firm to take over others by offering share certificates instead of cash to the sellers. These are very serious matters, for the serious take-over specialists have computerised tracking systems following every movement in the shares of their intended victims.

Quite clearly, the chairman needs to be able to understand his balance sheet, but he also needs to be briefed on what lies behind the figures. That would be done by an accountant, and the purpose of the briefings is to enable the chairman to anticipate and deal with any awkward questions, as well as to make play with successes. Hence the accountant concerned has to be well acquainted with the ways in which the City thinks. He may well find himself accompanying the chairman on these trips, especially if he is the finance director as well as an accountant.

In the smaller organisation the accountant will take on much of the job of representing the organisation to its owners and backers. He will probably be company secretary as well, and as guardian of its legal and fiscal propriety he is well suited to the task. The owners may be a small group of individuals – perhaps the family of the founders – and represent a very different set of interests from those exhibited at a large firm's AGM.

The accountant's dilemma

There is a whole series of balancing acts which the accountant is called upon to perform. If his colleagues fail to understand what they are and why it is important to resolve them, much internal dissension may be caused.

The more important dilemmas involve clashes between:

- accuracy and timeliness,
- paying suppliers or conserving cash,
- putting liquidity at risk or chasing customers for payment.

Accuracy clashes with timeliness in a most obvious way. If information is to be useful it must be provided in time to be understood and acted upon. That often means that it has to be produced at speed, and speed can mean inaccuracy. Every report has two parameters: the degree of accuracy necessary and the latest time by which it can usefully be supplied. In some cases a painstaking effort is needed because accuracy is more important than time: an example might be an investigation into alleged fraud on the computer system. In another situation speed might be all-important, a 'quick and dirty' reading being far more useful than a precise analysis that takes days to prepare. Into that category fall most of the requests for *ad hoc* help made by managers to enable them to see how things are going. They are really looking for a broad indication of whether or not things are going to plan, so that if the rough figure shows that things are more or less all right, they can turn their attention elsewhere; if it suggests that things might be going wrong, they can get more precise information on the area which seems to be the source of the trouble.

When it comes to the decision about whether to pay a supplier or to hold on to the cash, the accountant's first instinct is to keep the money. He realises that this cannot be done indefinitely, and that any undue delay would damage the relationship with suppliers on whom the firm depends. The safety mechanism which stops the accountant from withholding payment for too long is the pressure from colleagues whose suppliers refuse to make further deliveries until the account is up to date. Certain large organisations who believe that their clout allows them to get away with almost anything, deliberately hold on to such payments for at least three months. Few suppliers expect to be paid on delivery, but after six or eight weeks they feel that they ought to be paid. Thirteen weeks feels too much like exploitation, and they seek customers elsewhere. The irony is that the attempt to use suppliers' money to fund its own operations drives the big organisation's best suppliers away; and those who continue to sell to it raise their prices to compensate for the delay in payment. Does such a policy really pay off in the long run? Its attraction is that the money not paid out is equivalent to money not borrowed, so that interest costs are reduced, but the savings may prove to be illusory.

If the organisation hits an emergency shortage of cash, for a time few suppliers would get paid. Those who did would be the bare minimum of suppliers without whose goodwill the organisation could not function. They include the utilities and vital raw materials suppliers. Others could complain but they would not get paid until the crisis had passed. If it proved terminal, those suppliers would remain unpaid for at least a couple of years while liquidators dissected the corpse. A sudden change in payment habits can spell trouble, so credit managers watch out for such signs.

This brings us to the third of the accountant's dilemmas, that of balancing the need for liquidity against the danger of alienating customers by chasing them too hard for payment. In the normal course of events a compromise is worked out, with the sales people representing the customer's point of view. If the credit manager should suspect that the collapse of a customer may be imminent, he acts immediately. He threatens the customer with a writ or a winding-up petition, pointing out that this will be published in the media which credit managers read, and will trigger a flood of similar actions from other suppliers and hasten the downfall. That is not vindictive, it is simply making sure that if anyone is to be paid it is the credit manager's own firm.

That series of actions would be taken only by agreement with the sales department, who will have the responsibility for re-establishing the relationship if the customer survives the crisis. They also have a hand in setting the limit on the amount of credit allowed to customers, a flexible figure which is adjustable upwards if it hampers the development of the account, or downwards if the customer begins to look shaky.

Basic accounting concepts: cash flow forecasting

This is the first of a series of sections which looks at some of the ways in which accountants do their work.

The main immediate aim of any organisation must be to survive. The factor which governs survival (discounting voluntary discontinuance) is liquidity, the ability to pay bills as they fall due. An illiquid organisation may be rich, but the fact that its wealth is held in the form of (say) land means that it cannot pay its bills. Some of the wealth will have to be turned into cash before the creditors can be satisfied, and that takes time. The staff, the taxman and all the suppliers need to be paid in money, not title deeds.

Other issues of importance are profit and profitability (which are related but different). *Liquidity* will be dealt with first.

To the surprise of most people, accountants treat liquidity as being of greater importance than profit. They are quite right to do so, for an unprofitable firm can survive for quite a long time under normal circumstances, but one which is illiquid fails immediately. The item in the accountant's tool kit which enables him to predict liquidity is the cash flow forecast.

In principle, a cash flow forecast is very simple: most nine-year-olds have no trouble in understanding it, so the first-time manager should find it very easy indeed.

The aim of the cash flow forecast is to work out what the bank balance is likely to be at the end of each of a specified number of periods of time in the future say, monthly for the next year. The point of that is to see if, by operating in the way it plans to, the firm will run dangerously short of cash. If the forecast says it will, the action planned can be reviewed to see what changes to operational activity will bring about a less hazardous cash situation.

The calculation involved is simplicity itself:

- start with the cash in the bank now
- add the cash which ought to come in during the period (it is assumed here to be a month)
- subtract the cash likely to be paid out in the period
- the result is the cash which will be left over at the end of the month, if the earlier assumptions come true; this becomes the opening balance for the next month.

The process is then repeated until 11 periods in question have been covered. To anyone who has ever completed a stock record that process is familiar. Stock records start with the number of size 12 widgets in stock, add on those expected in, subtract those which will be used, and arrive at a month-end total. That figure becomes the opening balance for the following month, and the process is repeated. In the case of stock, a predetermined reorder level triggers the placing of replenishment orders, without which it would run out. In the case of cash, there is no certainty at the start that the supply will be exhausted, since the reservoir is being constantly topped up by incoming payments from customers. Instead of looking to see *when* the firm will run out of cash, the accountant is trying to find out *if* it will and if so, *when* and *to what extent*. If the extent is major, extra finance will be needed or the plans will have to change to a less cash-hungry mode of operation. If it is minor and temporary it could be covered by slowing down payments to suppliers, or a bank overdraft, or both.

A cash flow forecast for a large organisation is a complex-looking document, but the principles it follows are exactly those outlined above. The crucial point to remember is that a sale is recorded as such the moment the invoice is raised; it does not become *cash*, in the form in which it can be spent, until someone pays the bill – and that could be months later. Many commercial failures come about, especially in the small firms sector, because people think that they can spend against invoices issued, whereas they can in reality only against cash received.

The profit and loss account

The standard document which reports profits is the profit and loss account (P&L). A P&L is another basically simple document. It applies to a period of time, usually a year, and is created thus:

> Total value of invoiced sales,
> Subtract what was paid for things sold,
> = Gross profit.

> Subtract all the other expenses of actually running the firm,
> = Operating profit.

> Subtract cost of finance,
> = Net profit before tax.

> Subtract tax due on net profit before tax,
> = Net profit.

In that simple breakdown there appear four different definitions of 'profit'. Thus one of the first things the first-time manager learns is that when the word profit is used unqualified, he asks for the type of 'profit' to be defined.

Profitability is something else again. It is the measure of return on some resource. The profitability of a new investment is the rate at which it earns a profit. If it cost £100,000 and earns £40,000 a year, its profitability is 40 per cent. Typically, organisations are interested in ranking their activities in order of profitability, the more easily to distinguish the most rewarding from the least. Their calculation or calculations of profitability will be based on the scarcest or most expensive resources: there is nothing to stop the calculation from being performed many times on different bases. To take an example, a precision engineer with a highly skilled workforce may have invested heavily in computer-controlled machines. He will be interested in two key figures: the profitability of his very expensive investment and the profitability of his highly paid workforce. He will examine in detail what return he gets per pound invested, and per hour which his workforce operates. He may also wish to investigate the profitability of individual customers or groups and types of customers.

The balance sheet

The two standard documents used for reporting company results are the P&L and the balance sheet. The P&L shows what profit has been earned, which is an important part of the story of what has been done with the owner's money. The owner also wants to know what all his money is tied up in at the end of the reporting period: that is what the balance sheet tells him.

In order to create a balance sheet, the organisation freezes its transactions at a particular moment and records the position of all its assets and liabilities – the wealth it owns and the money it owes. That position is different both immediately beforehand and immediately afterwards. For that reason it is frequently described as a 'snapshot' of the organisation's funds.

The fundamental message conveyed by the balance sheet is twofold:

• how much money has been raised and from where
• where that money was tied up, or where it was lost to.

Strictly speaking, the quantities shown on a balance sheet represent wealth rather than money, but since accountancy depends on the use of the money measure for everything (see earlier in this chapter), that wealth is expressed in monetary terms. Two acres of industrial land is wealth in anybody's terms, and therefore has to be shown in the owner's balance sheet. Unfortunately he cannot show it as such in any accounting document, so it has to be converted into its estimated value, say £200,000. That enables the different forms of wealth to be totalled, whether they are in the form of stock, materials, equipment, vehicles, buildings, money owed to him or cash.

All this involves a certain amount of estimation, as has been mentioned already. It also means that the accountant closes his eyes to ways of looking at values which can be much more relevant in some circumstances. The idea of the 'going concern' has been touched on. It means that things are valued for accounting purposes on the assumption that the organisation will continue in business. Thus a half-completed car which is part-way through the factory is assumed to be saleable for a price which reflects the work put into it. If the firm really does continue in business that is the only realistic way of valuing that item, but suppose it is only days away from liquidation? The accountant would continue to value everything on the 'going concern' basis, even though the half-completed assemblies cramming the factory floor will be saleable only as scrap in a week's time. In such a situation, of course, nobody would delude themselves into thinking that the 'going concern' values are what the factory could be sold for. Under these conditions two parallel sets of valuations are done: the conventional one, and in addition a realistic assessment of what everything would fetch if the worst happened. The only valuation which means anything in the end is the price agreed between a willing buyer and a willing seller.

Mention of those different forms of assets introduces the distinction between fixed assets and current assets and their counterparts on the other side of the equation, long-term liabilities and current liabilities. Assets are things owned by an organisation or individual on which a money value can be placed under the conventions of accounting. Liabilities are their mirror image: the debts owed on which a money value is placed. In brief, fixed assets are the ones which the organisation intends to hang on to and to use, like buildings, vehicles and equipment. Current assets are those which it means to sell or otherwise recover the value of within a year, like stocks or debtors (money owed by customers, on the whole). As for liabilities, the short-term (current) ones are due for settlement within a year and the long-term ones, those which fall due later than that. In practice, many long-term liabilities remain outstanding for the entire life of the organisation.

The layout and meaning of a balance sheet are illustrated in simple form in Figure 26.

It is easy to jump to the conclusion that certain categories of asset are always treated as fixed assets. Machinery might be an example. The key to classification lies in the owner's intent. If he is a manufacturer, he intends to keep and use a machine for a number of years, so that it is certainly a fixed asset to him. A machinery dealer, however, would sell it as quickly as he could. Thus to him it is an item of his stock-in-trade, and thus a current asset.

At this stage it is worth stopping for a moment to consider what the balance sheet is saying. Its message is:

'We own fixed assets worth this much; add on the current assets, to see the value of all the assets we own; subtract from that what we owe in the short term, and see the total value of the investment in the firm; you can also see what it is tied up in. To see where the investment came from and in what form, look at the long-term liabilities.'

Heading		Usual contents
	Fixed assets	Plant, machinery, land, buildings, vehicles, equipment
(+)	Current assets	Cash, stock, money owed to us
(=)	Total assets	(ie everything we own)
(−)	Current liabilities	Debts for stock and day-to-day supplies, tax due shortly; short-term loans (eg overdrafts, which can be called-in without notice)
(=)	Net worth	(ie what we are worth when our immediate debts are subtracted from what we own)

[This completes the first part of the balance sheet, which shows where the money put into the organisation is tied up. It is followed by the part which shows where the money came from.]

	Long-term liabilities	Income from sale of shares; reserves created by profits (or reduction in worth caused by accumulated losses); long-term loans; longer-term tax liabilities

[Net worth and long-term liabilities are equal to each other. They have to be, since one shows where the money is now, the other shows where it came from.]

Figure 26 *The balance sheet simplified*

When the balance sheet is put together with the P&L, some very useful information emerges. The degree of risk of the firm failing can be pinpointed, as can the profitability of the assets, two factors of considerable interest to owners, managers and other employees. There is much else besides, a great deal of which is revealed by *ratio analysis*, a simple technique which involves examining the relationship between different items on the balance sheet and the P&L.

The first ratio which anyone looks at is the so-called *'acid test'* or *liquidity ratio*. That examines whether the firm is in a position to pay its bills as they fall due. It takes the items which are cash (or almost as good as cash, such as debts owed to the firm) to see if they total enough to meet the current liabilities. If they are in a relationship of at least 1:1, all is assumed to be well for the immediate future, although there must always be questions about who the debtors are and how old the debts. Doubtful categories would include money owed by people who have absconded or firms which have failed, as well as debts which are in dispute for reasons of non-compliance with contract terms or because nobody can substantiate an invoice with a signed delivery receipt. Some companies' accounts contain a horrifyingly high proportion of such debts. One manager who went to work for a small group found this out at first hand. He tells the story of finding about £250,000 owed to the firm, of which over £100,000 had been in dispute for over two years with half-a-dozen large customers. Thus nearly half the money that the firm ought apparently to be able to collect was simply not available, and unlikely ever to be collected.

The next test is the *current ratio*, in which current liabilities and current assets are compared. The point is to see if the firm will fail in the medium term. Accountants' experience shows that there ought generally to be at least £2 of current assets to £1 of current liabilities, to allow a comfortable margin of safety.

Having satisfied himself that the firm does not seem to be in immiment danger of collapse, the accountant might then look to see what return it is earning on the money invested in it. There is no single 'good' rate of return, since return ought to comprise two elements: the cost of the use of money (interest rate) which is more or less the same for all businesses, plus an amount which reflects risk. Since the latter is very variable between companies and markets there can be no all-embracing convention.

The large and sophisticated organisation is perfectly aware, of course, that these criteria are being used to judge its published results. For that reason many organisations choose to massage their year-end figures without actually lying. This is done by such techniques as placing a ban on buying stock or on capital expenditure for the last few weeks of the year. That allows stocks to fall and cash to build up, thus making the firm look more liquid. The trouble which that causes is twofold: once it has been done at all the trick has to be repeated every year, and it introduces inefficiencies which will affect next year's profit figures. Nevertheless, managements feel that they are driven to use such expedients by the constant pressure for results now which is placed on them by the City.

Gearing

Gearing is a term which the first-time manager will encounter at some time. Gearing relates to where the long-term funding has come from, recognising that loans are different from risk capital in the form of shares. The figures from which it is derived are all in the long-term liabilities part of the balance sheet. Gearing is the product of another ratio, that between the fixed capital, in the form of shares or owners' investment, and long-term loans. Its significance lies in the organisation's exposure to risk versus its ability to exploit favourable conditions quickly. If times are good, money costs 10 per cent and a 30 per cent return can be earned on it, it makes sense to borrow as much as you can and maximise earnings. If times are bad, the firm which makes no operating profit need not pay its shareholders (for that is one of the risks they take), yet it still has to pay interest on any loan. Thus in the good times earnings from heavily borrowed firms will be good, in bad times they will be poor – or even lead to the lenders calling in the loans, so that the firm collapses. Accountants like to see £1 of loan to £2 of equity (such a firm has a gearing of 33 per cent), or at most £1 to £1 (gearing of 50 per cent). A firm which has gearing of 10 per cent is said to have low gearing; one which is geared at 80 per cent is highly geared by anyone's standards.

The final word on the topic of ratios is that there is a multitude which can be calculated. The point is not just to do the arithmetic, but to select those which have meaning in the context of that firm's circumstances. They should produce information on the firm's internal position, its likely future performance and its relationship to comparable and competing firms as a way of judging its management. Particularly revealing are changes over time.

Sources and application of funds

Recognising the importance attached to the question of organisational liquidity, companies are increasingly showing a further table in their annual reports, a sources and applications of funds statement (S&A). Accountants and others in the know have always been able to work this out for themselves from the other documents, but this labour-saving approach is welcomed by all. The first-time manager will do well to pay attention to that report, for it discloses early signals to changes in the health of the firm by way of that vital measure, liquidity.

What the S&A does is a simple piece of arithmetic. In essence, it takes the balance sheets for the start and the end of the year, and calculates the changes in the size of each item. A reduction of stock, for instance, is represented by an increase in liquidity, a reduction in cash a decrease. The question which it answers is: 'Where have changes in funds come from in the year, and what have they been tied up in?'

Costing

This is a subject on which books the size of door-stops have been written. Cost accounting is an important discipline in its own right, as well as a key element in the art and science of management accounting. Its concern is to identify what the true expression is in money terms of everything done in the organisation, so that nobody deludes themselves about the implications of their actions. It is a vital aid to management, and probably its most important contribution comes in telling what the organisation's products really cost.

The cost accountant starts by classifying costs into categories. The first level of classification is by function, for example whether a cost properly lies with the production function or the distribution function. Within these functions it establishes cost centres, places where a group of people works together (or any other useful unit) for which costs can be gathered. They might include the training department, the London warehouse, or the retailing division.

Next comes the idea of the 'cost unit', the unit of output to which all these costs are to be attached. For a civil engineering firm it might be a particular motorway contract, or for a food manufacturer canned beans size A2.

All the costs which a firm incurs fall into three categories: materials, including sub-assemblies and components; payroll; and general outgoings like premises, fuel, depreciation, utilities and interest. Further, they are either 'direct' or 'indirect'. Direct ones are clearly identifiable as belonging to a cost unit – the distribution department's diesel for instance. Indirect costs cannot be readily identified as having an 'owner', such as the rental of the telex which everyone uses, or the interest on long-term loans. Having said that, the cost accountant is constantly at war with the imprecision which indirect costs suggest. He longs to find a home in a cost unit somewhere for every one of these motherless waifs. Nevertheless, the common sense with which he is liberally endowed tells him that there is always an irreducible minimum which no existing cost unit ought to be asked to absorb, and for which no cost unit can reasonably be created. He is therefore under constant pressure from the managers of cost centres to share out a cost which they feel ought not to be borne entirely by them.

Some of the biggest problems faced by the cost accountant have to do with apportioning indirect costs to the individual products or cost units. The distribution department is a cost centre in its own right, but its costs can be met only by the profit centres (yes, there are those too) which actually sell the firm's output. If a parcels carrier were to deliver every item sold, there would be little problem: each case of product would be charged for individually and the costs could be allocated accordingly. When the firm's own lorries make the deliveries the share to be borne by each product is less clear-cut.

Firms therefore apply some convention, based on the limiting factor. If the product is feather quilts, it will be the space on the lorries and each product will be charged a proportion of the costs based on the volume shipped. If it is steel strip, the limiting factor on the lorries' loads will be weight. Thus the share of costs will be the share of the total weight delivered. Where, as so often happens, the products come in a variety of densities, the choice of system for allocating cost can be crucial.

As an example, a firm makes two products: boxes and blocks. The same number of units is sold of each, but one block is five times the weight of a box. The block is also a quarter of the volume of a box. The characteristics of the distribution task are as follows:

	Boxes	Blocks
Weight (kg)	2	10
Volume (litres)	20	5
Number sold	1,000	1,000
Total weight (kg)	2,000	10,000
Total volume (litres)	20,000	5,000

Thus the firm has to ship 2000 items a year which weigh 12,000 kg and occupy 25,000 litres. It costs £50,000 a year to run the delivery function, and the cost accountant has to consider how best to allocate the cost. He does some arithmetic:

	Boxes	Blocks
Cost per unit if apportioned by:		
Weight:	£8	£42
Volume:	£40	£10
Numerical share of deliveries:	£25	£25

This shows that the cost per unit could vary wildly, depending on the costing basis selected. This is important because the one he picks could dramatically alter the pricing of the product and thus its chances of survival in the market-place and in the firm's range of products. Thus the wrong decision here could even result ultimately in the closure of a factory, with all the appalling effects that can have. In the end, under this example, the accountant would probably plump for a cost per unit based on some combination of volume and weight effects, but the decision is neither clear-cut nor easy. This highlights the difficulty associated with the technique of *absorption costing*, the method which tries to load on to each product a share of central overheads. What may have originally been fairly arbitrary decisions over how indirect costs are to be apportioned can assume major importance when decisions are being taken over which products are too unprofitable to continue with. It can be downright dangerous when pricing is under discussion, and it is inflexible in the face of variations in the underlying assumptions about costs and volumes.

To address that difficulty the idea of 'contribution' was developed. Instead of trying to share out all the indirect costs, just the direct costs are allocated to each product. They are subtracted from the selling price to produce the contribution (ie to indirect costs and, it is hoped, profit). The total of all the contributions over the year from all the products is then set against the total of the indirect costs, and anything left over is profit. Clearly that is a lot simpler and more flexible, but it does mean that even greater vigilance is needed. It is vital that good systems exist for tracking the actual contribution compared to plan, since a loss of volume from a high contributor could, if not spotted and acted upon, plunge the firm into loss.

The test of costing decisions is with hindsight, when it becomes clear whether or not the product is over or under priced, and whether or not the volumes expected were sold at a price which allowed recovery of the actual indirect costs of running the business.

A general principle in accounting is that, if total profit is to be maximised, the profit on each unit of the scarcest resource must be maximised. In other words, the bottleneck which is stopping things from expanding or speeding up has to be identified. The most profitable item or mix of items which can be sold is that which produces the greatest return from the use of the bottleneck resource. If the lorry fleet is the limiting factor, and suppose that the firm makes £20 profit on all items in its range, it will make the biggest profit by cramming the lorries with the smallest item of all and delivering none of the biggest. In that way it maximises the number of £20s it makes. More often that profit will be expressed as contribution, since it is not yet, strictly speaking, profit at all. The scarce resource varies from organisation to organisation, but knowing which it is and squeezing as much out of it as possible is a very important management task.

Thus there is no one costing system suitable for all firms in all situations. Even the custom-built system is likely to be just the best compromise available rather than perfect in every detail, despite the fact that an enormous amount of thought will have been expended on its design.

The mention of contribution brings in the idea of *marginal costing*. A firm needs to know what is the lowest price for which its products can sell without actually incurring a loss. That knowledge enables it to set a floor price below which no sale must ever be made, and to negotiate against if there is ever the opportunity to fill some vacant capacity at a low selling price. The marginal cost of a product is the cost of selling one extra item once all the indirect costs have been covered by the rest of the output. Its use must be carefully controlled since, if the other costs are not fully met, the marginal cost will certainly not meet them.

Another concept which the cost accountant has constantly in mind is that of *opportunity cost*. It is the idea that one of the costs of doing what we are doing now is the sacrifice of the opportunity of doing something else. In practical terms, if a firm does something which earns it £20,000 instead of something which would earn it £30,000, the opportunity cost of that decision is £10,000. Or if research expenditure rises by £100,000 it is at an opportunity cost to all sorts of activities, including to shareholders' dividends of £100,000.

Break-even analysis

A firm knows that its capacity will sometimes not be completely filled. The level of sales may be able to fall some way without eliminating profit; the question is, by how much?

The break-even chart illustrates this clearly, and also shows how much profit or loss will be made at different levels of output. Figure 27 shows that it comprises three elements: the levels of fixed costs (similar to the indirect costs discussed above), variable costs (similar to direct costs) and sales. Fixed and variable costs are combined to show total costs, and when this is compared to the income from sales the level of output at which the firm breaks even can easily be seen.

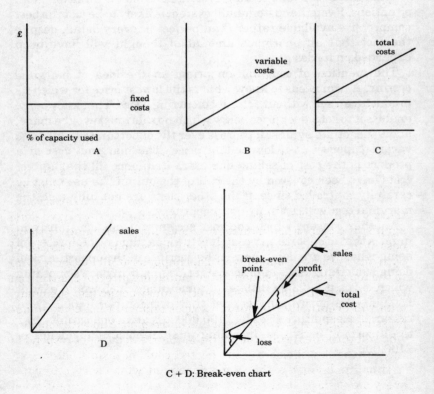

C + D: Break-even chart

Figure 27 *Break-even analysis*

190

Budgeting

One of the accountant's main jobs is to help with the setting of budgets and monitoring performance against them. A budget, in these terms, is a financial plan which shows what revenues are expected, what expenditures have been allowed for and hence what profit or loss is anticipated. As has been mentioned, the entire process usually starts from the creation of a sales forecast, and goes on to working out the cost of servicing that level of sales. To a sales manager, for example, the financial budget lays down two important goals: the value of sales which he is expected to achieve, and the amount of expense which he is expected not to exceed in the course of gaining them. He will also have operating budgets which translate the value of the sales figures into volumes of particular products. The figures will be no strangers to him since he will have been instrumental in their creation. It is a prime principle of budgeting that the managers who have to carry out the plans create the budgets. If budgeting is left to some central function, the operating managers can scarcely be blamed if they refuse to accept responsibility for achieving them. A budget which nobody is trying to achieve has no reason to exist, for the whole point of it is to create an overall plan for the period concerned which, ideally, everyone achieves exactly. Of course, there are always over- and under-achievers, but the existence of the budget enables top management to see whether or not variances are important.

Budgets are created for all the cost and profit centres, to give those responsible for them a precise statement of what they are expected to achieve. They are also fed with reports from the accountants which show at the end of each month how they have done against the plan. Each manager reviews his performance with his boss at the end of each month and formulates what he will do to deal with any variance from budget. This happens at all levels right up to the top of the organisation. If the managing director is sitting on an organisation which is persistently under-achieving, the chairman will eventually run out of excuses and will then come under pressure from investors to unseat him and replace him with someone who will turn the results round. If the chairman does not respond in the way the shareholders desire he, too, could be dismissed.

Thus the budget is the single document which serves to point everyone's efforts in the same direction, causing the organisation to work as a cohesive whole rather than as a collection of individuals each with their own personal aims to achieve.

Project evaluation

When the manager is confronted by the possibility of spending money now for an expected return later, the accountants become involved in evaluating the project. Given that one of the scarcest resources in any organisation is usually money, they are concerned that only the projects which give the best return should attract investment.

The three usual ways of looking at investments and their likely returns are ones which compute the speed at which the investment will be paid back, a computation of the annual rate of return, and a calculation of the project's discounted cash flow.

The *payback* method asks: 'How long before the initial investment is paid back from the savings or extra profits which it will generate?' In a small organisation in which most of the investments will pay themselves back in a year or so this might be acceptable. It is not adequate elsewhere, as will be discussed.

The *annual rate of return* asks a similar question: 'What annual percentage return on the investment do the savings or extra profits yield?' Again this method is deficient in the case of the project from which the savings will not recover its costs more or less straight away.

The problems with these approaches spring from two sources. One is that both of them place the same value of savings made today as those made in a year's, or five years', time. To offset the change in the real value of money an inflation factor can be applied; the effect is real enough as can be seen from this table:

Present value of £1, discounted at 10 per cent pa

Today	After	1 year	2 years	3 years
£1		90p	81p	73p ... and so on

Even where a discounting factor is applied the methods are deficient. They fail to distinguish between the profit arising from the investment and the cash flow pattern which it implies. As we have seen, it is perfectly possible to bankrupt yourself in pursuit of a profitable project which runs you out of cash. Thus the primacy of cash flow must be recognised in any evaluation of investment projects.

To allow cash flows to be taken into account, as well as the time-value of money, the method known as discounted cash flow (DCF) was developed. To take a simple illustration, an investment of £10 will create savings of £2 a year, and annual inflation of 10 per cent is expected. The DCF calculation looks like this:

Year:	1	2	3	4	5
Outflows	£10	–	–	–	–
Inflows	£2	£1.80	£1.62	£1.46	£1.31
Net flow	(£8)	£1.80	£1.62	£1.46	£1.31
– Cumulative	(£8)	(£6.20)	(£4.58)	(£3.12)	(£1.81)

Thus the organisation has to be able to fund an outflow in today's money of £8 this year: if it can do that, the benefits are shown in future years. If it could not do it then it will look elsewhere to invest. The payback method would say that it will be paid off in four years. The rate of return calculation shows that the investment is earning 25 per cent a year. By contrast DCF has shown that the initial outflow still has not been recouped after five years: indeed, it will not be recovered fully until part-way through year 7. The advantage of this method becomes most apparent when the outflows go on for quite a while before any return comes in, quite a familiar pattern for many in big industry. DCF paints the flows in full Technicolor horror, so that there is no confusion between the glowing reports of potential profit and the certainty of imminent cash outflows.

No single technique tells the manager or the accountant all that they need to know, but DCF comes nearest to universal acceptance.

Chapter 8
Personnel

Why personnel departments exist

The organisation's personnel department deals with its most important resource, people. Yet personnel departments are often scorned by operating managers who see their sole utility as welfare workers among pensioners and the sick. They also see personnel departments as an expensive luxury which have the cheek to try to build empires. Indeed, the first to be fired from a new acquisition by the takeover specialists are said to be the personnel people.

It is tempting to think that personnel departments which attract such derision have only themselves to blame. Where personnel work is seen in its true light, the people in that function are excellent: is it the commitment to effective but humane management which creates an insistence on a superb personnel department, or is it first-rate personnel managers who earn respect for the contribution they make? Certainly colleagues' valuation of their work will colour the judgement made of any personnel department; but the commitment to excellence in that department has to be made by top management in order for it to come about. If personnel work is seen as a low-level activity, the chances are that the jobs in that department will be low-grade and will attract people who would be relatively ineffective in any function.

The true work of a personnel department is very rarely practised in Britain today. It is to enable the organisation to get the best performance, short- and long-term, out of that contrary and difficult – but completely indispensable – resource, people.

Those who go into personnel work do so for many reasons. One is that they harbour feelings of goodwill towards their fellow humans, enjoy dealing with them and would like to improve their lot. There is nothing wrong with that, and a lot that is admirable about it.

However, the realities of personnel work can often conflict with this ethos of goodwill. For a start, personnel people can find themselves being expected to manipulate colleagues towards ends defined by greedy, uncaring and selfish managers. In those circumstances the personnel manager can either refuse and get the sack, walk out in disgust and lose his income, or stay. Most are forced to do the last.

Most operating managers will confess in moments of frankness that they are not quite sure why their organisation bothers to employ a personnel department. They see their personnel colleagues as a bunch of refugees from real life, who have fled from the world of action, responsibility, accountability and precision which the operating manager inhabits. In their place the personnel manager erects, they believe, a smokescreen of waffle about human relationships and personal development, founded on pop psychology.

The good personnel manager resists the implied suggestion that little or no account need be taken of people's legitimate human needs. Indeed, he sees such talk as conclusive evidence of the size of the task he faces in bringing the gospel to these heathen. He will feel at no disadvantage to his colleagues, for he will have proved himself in the heat of battle as an operating manager. He recognises the two challenges before him: to become such a useful and helpful staff manager that his colleagues will actively seek his advice rather than having to be force-fed it; and to introduce the floggers and hangers to the sides of human nature which respond to encouragement and help. In tackling either he is taking on a major task, to undertake both is either heroic or foolish. Nonetheless the good personnel manager tackles both and succeeds.

The personnel department can be a classic depository for all the unpopular tasks with no obvious home. Organising the staff Christmas dinner may be one, and a job out of which it is possible to make no friends and a large number of enemies. Firing people is another job which is uncongenial to anyone who is not psychopathic, and which is therefore sometimes passed to the personnel manager to undertake. If he accepts it both he and the person who wants it done have greatly misunderstood the part that personnel management plays in relation to disciplinary matters.

The personnel department and discipline

The first mistake in that process is that staff and line functions have become confused. The line (operating) manager is directly responsible for recruiting, motivating and disciplining his staff. The employee cannot be expected to be responsible to his manager for his output and to the personnel department for disciplinary issues. Therefore no personnel manager worth his salt would dream of interposing himself between the employee and his boss. None the less, he has responsibilities to the organisation. He would remind the manager of the company policy, the letter of the law and considerations of best practice to ensure consistency and fairness in the way employees are treated. Thus he might be consulted about the decision to dismiss and be present at any interview towards that end, but he ought not to carry out the dismissal itself.

It is in the disciplinary area that personnel people have some of their most unpleasant experiences, but they owe allegiance to the organisation which pays them to put their technical expertise to work in its interest. An operating manager has problems with a subordinate and invokes the disciplinary procedure (every firm must have one). It may be in the operating manager's mind to get rid of a difficult employee, but he knows that he has to do it within the rules. He looks to the personnel department to collude with him in dismissing this person. If the personnel manager suspects that there may be more personal animus than evidence of poor work, he is in a difficult position. Ideally, the manager would be shown the error of his ways and would reform: the people, the department and the organisation would gain from a switch out of negativism and into a positive concern to help the employee to contribute properly. On occasion, an analysis of the situation by the personnel manager will bring about this change of approach. Regrettably it does not always work. In some cases the operating manager is in a position of vastly greater power than the personnel person. The personnel manager may then have to choose between standing up for his beliefs or selling out his principles in order to stay employed.

An extreme example was chosen in that illustration, where someone stood to lose his job. The pressures to conform to the operating manager's requirements are just as strong where mere manipulation is concerned. The personnel manager may be expected to join in bullying or persuasion in order to get someone to do something he does not like the sound of.

The personnel department's proper contribution

The departmental power balance is in better equilibrium where the organisation recognises from the top that personnel issues have the importance that they really do carry. For a start, the organisation's culture reflects the strong concern to develop and enable rather than coerce and enforce. Then a superior type of manager will be recruited to run the department, which might even be represented at board level. It will not only be supported in its efforts to raise the general standard of the management of people throughout the organisation, it will also be positively required to do so. Such is the strength of the cultural dimension that no manager will take any decision without considering its implications for people. To ensure that he has thought them through fully, he will automatically lay his thoughts before the personnel people to get their reactions. Everything will be done to ensure that the organisation gets the best possible return on the vital human resource.

Personnel departments which operate in the latter type of environment find themselves moving in a virtuous circle. The support which the culture gives them lends weight to their views; the better quality personnel people apply to work for that organisation; line managers receive service which develops their respect for personnel work; and the culture recognises even more strongly the importance of the personnel department's contribution.

What the personnel department does

Its overall role
The guidance which a personnel department gives to line managers improves their handling of their people, and thus helps them to become better, more rounded managers. By encouraging a manager to think of the wider effects on people of his actions, the personnel operator is acting as midwife to the line manager's self-development. Dealing with real issues at his own desk, assisted by an expert, is no less valuable a way of learning than going on courses.

Recruitment
The specialist contribution of the personnel department is particularly valuable in helping the organisation to recruit, train and retain good people. Those broad headings encompass many individual activities and the exercise of a number of skills.

197

The job of finding good people starts well before the recruitment ads appear. The first step is to ensure that the organisation presents a face to the world which is attractive to the kind of people it wishes to employ. In that task the personnel department may work closely with PR people. Just as the way the organisation looks to customers is too important to be left to chance, so the enlightened personnel operator will try to ensure that all potential employees have a favourable impression of the organisation as an employer. It will lay particular stress on certain groups of key workers without a good supply of which it could not fulfil its aims. A software firm, for instance, may not be able to grow unless it recruits and keeps the right sort of systems designers. It will therefore take particular care to see that it is projected as an interesting, informal organisation offering many varied challenges and opportunities in more than one field. It will try hard to ensure that it is not seen as rigid, fuddy-duddy and class-ridden, for those values are anathema to the kind of people it needs. To shift to another example, a City organisation which prided itself in its traditionalism and respect for probity would not want to recruit somebody with the sharpest commercial instincts. Neither side would enjoy the brief period of mutual exasperation which would precede the inevitable separation. Yet that person would have a real contribution to make elsewhere in the City, perhaps as a dealer in a fast-moving trading market. The person is not wrong as such, simply right for one environment and not for another. In deciding how to project the organisation, a study of its competitors for the same scarce manpower resources will be held, for nothing like this can be done in a vacuum.

Communications

The personnel department is therefore often in the position of conducting its own communications campaign on behalf of the organisation to potential employees. The message cannot fail to be picked up by existing staff as well. That is no accident, for it does no harm to bring home to them that they could find worse employers. It also highlights the need to stray as little as possible from the truth about working conditions.

The techniques employed include:

- placing articles by employees in suitable media
- sponsorships and support of charities, professional institutes and industry organisations
- encouraging academic study of the organisation

- presence at careers exhibitions, in suitable directories and other media.

Articles for the media can be on virtually any aspect of organisational life. The staff who write them gain in professional standing, and the organisation gains by association. They might even be articles by the personnel department itself. Under the same general heading is the offer to the media of expert interviewees who can be called on at short notice to comment on anything from the effects of the Budget to technical advances in the industry.

Community involvement not only shows the firm in a good light but it allows the wider world to look at its people as human beings as well as office-holders. The bodies and activities with which the organisation chooses to associate itself in this way need to be picked with care. They ought to be consistent with the image which the organisation wishes to project, and should harmonise with its values and practices. It reinforces perceptions of leadership to see an organisation involved with the sponsorship of students at college, with the development of professional institutes and trade organisations, and helping appropriate charities.

Sponsorship of academic study can take a wide variety of forms, from endowing a chair at a leading university to allowing students to use the organisation as a guinea-pig for their projects. Academic involvement should carry a warning for the unwary, for once intelligent, motivated people are let loose they cannot be stopped from asking the questions which employees know are too sensitive to be referred to publicly. So if the MD's wife really does take all the decisions about the colour the products should be, design students ought to be kept away, if the personnel people value their jobs. Unless the lady in question is a professional designer, of course.

It must always be remembered that the values of the academic world are such that the results of research are published openly (though names can be withheld), whereas consultancy is confidential. To be anonymous in research publications is small consolation to the one manufacturer of grommets within 50 miles of Manchester who bares all, and finds himself described as a 'grommet maker in south-east Lancashire': anonymous, but identifiable. Two sides of the same question are involved here: the findings of the research could make the organisation look foolish, although it will draw its attention to things that urgently need putting right; and the fact of allowing the researchers in suggests a certain self-confidence tempered with humility. Organisations hope that the latter is the effect that will dominate, reinforcing perceptions that it offers a sympathetic environment in which to work.

There are famous cases of otherwise little-known organisations which are so well documented in the research literature that anyone who has studied organisations to any extent feels that he knows them fairly intimately. The effect can work in reverse, however. A company formed in the late 1960s was the subject of a Harvard Business School case study which appears unfailingly on most advanced management courses. It appears from the facts advanced as rather bumbling, yet the reverse was the case: after about 25 years' existence the founders sold out for £85 million, scarcely the sign of ineffective entrepreneurship.

External relationships
Perhaps the most obvious instance of image communication is at careers exhibitions, especially those on the 'milk round', on which recruiters visit the major universities to try to attract the brightest performers to join their graduate entry programmes. Professional help from specialists in communication is usually called in so as to create the very best appearance and overall impression.

The good personnel department realises that every single contact with its potential recruits may be a matter of routine to the managers concerned, but is considered very critically by the recruits themselves. For that reason they are painstaking about the form of words used in telephone conversations, face to face and in letters by themselves and their staff. This is a particularly sensitive issue when people are being refused an interview or are having their appplication turned down. The person who is treated unthinkingly at that point may form an unfavourable impression of the organisation. That may not matter too much for the immediate future, but in ten years' time he or she may be a highly desirable catch.

Recruitment advertising, interviewing and selection
Recruitment advertising can be directed along a number of routes. It can comprise ads placed in the press by the organisation itself, or ads placed on its behalf by recruitment agencies. Those agencies can also be briefed to examine the lists of potentially mobile staff which they hold. The technique of headhunting can be added where a key and probably senior appointment is being considered. Once again great attention will be paid to detail. Where agencies are involved the briefing to them will be carefully prepared and

delivered. Their enthusiasm for the organisation as an employer will be developed.

Once the advertising begins to attract replies, the response mechanism goes into action. All the means of handling replies will have been planned in advance, and the criteria for selecting interviewees agreed. This must all be done carefully yet at some speed, for an application which goes cold can be difficult to reactivate.

Interviewing is an art and a science all on its own. Good personnel people will be trained not only to ask the right questions but to listen to, judge and follow up the responses. The personnel department will be able to organise the structure and method of interview, and to ensure that the employing managers (the personnel department's clients) stick to them.

Following interview a decision has to be taken. Are any of the candidates worth recruiting? Which ones? What offers should be made? Should the second choices be told now, or should we wait until acceptance or rejection of the offers made by the first-choice candidate? These and other issues the personnel specialist will advise on. Not the least decision is whether or not to re-interview a shortlist in greater depth before deciding finally, though that would preferably have been decided as part of the initial planning of the process.

After a candidate has accepted in principle there will be negotiations over the details of the terms of the employment contract, pension rights, relocation expenses, company vehicle use and so forth. Again the personnel department will be involved. Then the new recruit joins, and one of his earliest contacts on the first day is with the personnel people who will exercise their standard induction procedure for new staff. That process is not accidental either, but is designed to cover in a logical order all the things he needs to know as a new member of the club.

Performance review

The employee, once recruited, will have his performance reviewed by his boss from time to time and his progress monitored by the personnel department. The procedure for this will have been designed by the personnel people in consultation with line managers. The point of performance review is that it helps the individual to know where he stands and to take appropriate action to improve his performance; the reason for monitoring it over a period is twofold. It enables tracking of the development of the individual, and it allows general conclusions to be drawn about the effectiveness of departments and of the organisation as a whole in creating the pool of skills and talent which it needs now and will need in the future. If there is strong disagreement between the employee and his boss about the conclusions the latter is coming to, the right of appeal to a higher level exists. That might be invoked only after the personnel department's attempts to arbitrate had failed.

The head of a section or of a department is called upon to be peculiarly unselfish. If he has a good member of his staff he relies on him, but he is expected to push him forward for promotion which may well mean that he is lost to another department. It is important that some mechanism should exist to ensure that good people are encouraged to help the organisation as well as themselves by exploring their potential to the full, rather than leaving in frustration to take up opportunities elsewhere. That is why the personnel department has to become involved in both career development and organisation development. It looks ahead to foresee future needs for people, and looks at the present people to assess their suitability and potential. It therefore becomes instrumental in shaping the pattern of jobs which the individual manager is invited to take on.

Trade unions

Another quite separate area of personnel responsibility is that of trade union negotiation. A major organisation with a unionised workforce knows for certain that the trade union will put up professional negotiators who are wily, tough and skilled at throwing their adversary off balance. If the organisation is not to find itself at a massive disadvantage it must match the trade union with negotiators of at least similar quality. Contrary to the popular belief, most trade unions are not ready to invoke the strike weapon at the drop of a hat. They know perfectly well that the long-term interests of their members lie with flourishing employers. They also know that they will forfeit the confidence of their membership if they do not get the maximum possible share of the resulting prosperity in the form of employee rewards, conditions and benefits. As part of their attempts to deal with that pressure they will try to depress members' expectations of what is possible so that what they come out with looks more like a victory. A 10 per cent rise when 15 per cent was expected looks like failure; if the expectation was for 5 per cent it can be perceived as a triumph. That can be difficult to engineer, especially when the union tests management's mettle with a well-publicised initial claim for 25 per cent.

Most contact with unions does not involve major issues like pay and conditions bargaining. The day-to-day work in organisations of representing union members' interests is done by those representatives elected from the workforce, the shop stewards. They raise routine grievances with management and will usually achieve a resolution. If matters escalate, the full-time union branch secretary may be called in to lend weight. The shop stewards' ready access to management levels and the implied threat of calling in the full-time union heavyweights does tend to undermine the position of the first-line supervisor or foreman. Nominally responsible for what is going on in his section he can find himself by-passed by direct approaches above his head.

Manpower planning

Personnel managers are responsible for ensuring that there will be an adequate supply available at the right time of people with the right characteristics to deal with the challenges expected to confront the organisation. It would clearly present major difficulties if, for instance, a major organisation experienced a hiatus of talent suitable to man its operations properly. To ensure that they get early warning of potential problems of that sort organisations employ manpower planning techniques.

In essence this is a stock control exercise: who there is to start with, plus who will be recruited, less who will leave or retire, equals who will be left. The workforce can be split in several ways for this examination. Individual departments and disciplines will be looked at, as will particular levels across the organisation as a whole. Any gaps revealed by comparison with the forecast of what numbers and skills will be needed can be met by either recruitment or training. The situation does not stand still for, unlike those classic subjects of stock control, widgets, the human resource develops and changes throughout its life-span. Nevertheless a sophisticated model can be built to take account of at least the major variable. It does not obviate all the difficulties, shortages or surpluses, but it does make many of them foreseeable and thus easier to deal with in a calm and controlled way.

Training

Training is another area of concern to personnel managers. Its purpose is to establish suitable levels of performance in the workforce and to maintain and amend them as requirements change. Change is the one fact of organisational life that is certain, and as an inescapable consequence organisations have to be prepared to train. Some people at all levels will be the sort of self-motivated individuals who get on with adapting themselves to the changes they see going around them. They are the people who, when computers began to take off in the late 1970s, saw their potential and bought their own to learn something about them. Modest though the home machines were at that time, the insights which their owners gained during long evenings of wrestling with programming problems taught them more than most of their contemporaries will ever learn on official courses. Most people do not have that sort of motivation, so the organisation finds that it has to take the initiative to identify training needs and design suitable responses to them. The range of training methods and vehicles to deal with different situations is vast, and requires specialist knowledge if they are to be employed properly. The personnel department does not carry out these evaluations and selections entirely alone, but in conjunction with its client departments.

Teams and personalities

Personnel managers also know that organisations are run not by individuals but by teams. Teams operate throughout organisations at all levels. By definition, they consist of different individuals. It may be that two or more members of a team are at one another's throats, so that any good work that might have been done is submerged beneath the infighting and quarrelling. There is quite a good chance that if the selection of team members is left to chance, there will be more friction. Instead the personnel department tries to understand the personality type and motivation of people likely to become involved in team work and advise those assembling them on how to avoid destructive tensions. For that reason the person best qualified to do the job is sometimes passed over in favour of somebody who will fit better into the set-up. That does not mean that teams must always be bland. There is a strong case for including that uncomfortable character who voices the unpopular view and dares to think and say the unthinkable. It avoids the tendency to 'groupthink' which crops up in many teams. There are occasions when it is right to introduce such an element in order to jolt a team into action. The point is that these teams ought to work best when they have been deliberately designed for the task they are to undertake, rather than thrown together willy-nilly.

A wide variety of tests is available which purport to identify and classify the personality-type of an individual. Managers have mixed feelings about them, mostly tinged by a degree of scepticism. Most agree that they do ring uncannily true on occasion, but the main objections to them are held quite strongly. They can be seen as an invasion of privacy; the amateur interpretation of the results is viewed with suspicion; and their results can in any case be distorted by anybody who has read the subversive guides on how to fiddle the answers to produce a particular outcome.

The personnel department therefore has wide-ranging responsibilities in relation to the organisation as a whole and to the individuals within it. Its work is never-ending, for no sooner has it dealt with a problem in one area than another pops up somewhere else. Overlaid on those short-term effects are the longer-term results of great shifts in society. One which has greatly affected whole organisations' philosophies of how they relate to their people, and hence to the work of personnel departments, is that which took place between 1979 and the late 1980s. Where beforehand many managements had been retreating before trade union aggression, later they asserted management's right to manage. Little enough was said about the responsibilities attaching to that right (except by a few enlightened leaders). The work of adjusting personnel policies to the constant shifts in the organisation's development in relation to internal pressures and the outside environment is a continuous task.

Personnel and the law

Ever since the industrial revolution matured, the law has concerned itself with matters related to employment. Child labour and safety in workplaces were obvious examples of areas in which appalling abuses brought about general revulsion and a determination to act.

The main areas of regulation with which personnel departments are concerned today concern:

- contracts of employment
- employment protection
- health and safety.

Health and safety legislation was always piecemeal until it was consolidated in the 1970s into a form which dealt not only with particular situations in individual industries, but also with a blanket insistence that work should be done in a safe manner. For the first time all employees in every industry were required to work safely.

205

Along with that came many detailed requirements on employers, from the labelling of containers to the appointment of safety representatives within each department. Most of the burden of understanding the detailed implications fell on personnel departments, who interpreted for colleagues and ensured compliance.

Written confirmation of the terms of an employment became required legally in the 1970s. While prudent and well-organised employers had always confirmed in writing the details of the relationship between them and their staff, the majority had never done so. Thus there was much room for misinterpretation and misunderstanding. The written details of the contract have to contain specified information on all the obvious matters like pay, hours, place of work, holiday entitlement, holiday pay, periods of notice and so forth. Good practice ties all those details in with company rules, job descriptions and grievance procedures.

The wise employer confirms to the employee in writing what the job comprises, to which post his job reports and which posts report to him. That document is referred to as a job description. There will also be company rules defining privileges, duties and unacceptable types of behaviour. Infractions must, by law, be dealt with by a formal disciplinary procedure. This will probably involve a temporary black mark on a person's file for small offences (such as lateness), right through to instant dismissal for bad behaviour such as working unsafely, violence or theft. The sensible personnel manager always invokes suspension so as to allow tempers to cool and evidence to be gathered before dismissal is effected.

Just as the employer must set up these formal procedures for disciplining the workers, so employees must have, again by law, the right to take up formally any grievances in connection with their employment. Grievance procedures generally expect difficulties to be resolved between the employee and his immediate superior, with appeal to higher levels if they cannot agree.

The ultimate arena for settling an employee's disputes with an employer is the industrial tribunal. It comprises three people, usually with a solicitor in the chair. Evidence is taken informally and awards can be made against the employer of costs and damages, or reinstatement in his job of the employee. Alternatively the employee may have to pay the employer's costs. No case reaches the industrial tribunal unless ACAS (Advisory, Conciliation and Arbitration Service, a government body) has tried and failed to bring about a settlement by negotiation.

Employment protection is such that, after working for one year for a large concern (two for a very small one) an employee cannot be rightfully dismissed arbitrarily. Furthermore, there is no qualifying period if the dismissal is on grounds of race or sex discrimination or pregnancy. He or she could be made redundant according to strict rules which test that the job, not just the individual's tenure of it, has been abolished. It is not that straightforward for the employer, as he is required to make a reasonable offer of work elsewhere, or pay compensation.

The risk that an employer might be called before an industrial tribunal stresses the need to keep records. All that falls to the personnel department to create, and often they have to maintain the records, although they will usually train the operating departments to keep them themselves. In tandem with recording events in relation to people's employment goes the need to train all levels of management from supervisor upwards in the duties which they and the organisation have under employment and safety legislation. Thus, in addition to the other demands on them, the personnel people have to be lawyers, administrators and trainers. Theirs is a demanding and fascinating calling.

Chapter 9
Self-Development

Where are you going?

By landing his present appointment the first-time manager has
already displayed a degree of ambition. In order to be sure of
making a real success of this job he should pay some attention to
acquiring skills and developing as a human being. The present job
may well be the pinnacle of his ambition for the time being, but that
feeling is unlikely to last for ever. In order to fit himself for bigger
challenges and greater responsibilities he ought to begin the
process of deepening and broadening his experience straight away.

The first thing he needs to decide is what his personal aims are. A
clear picture of the goal is essential if the shortest route is to be
taken to it. Once the objective has been named, the route to it and a
likely timetable become much clearer.

Some people have a well-defined sense of personal mission from
an early age. One manager recalls the girl he used to sit next to in
the village school, who impressed and confused the whole class of
eight-year-olds by declaring her intention to be a barrister – they
didn't even know what the word meant. Such ambitions can be
implanted by parents, or can be the product of fantasy like the boy's
dream of being an engine driver. Parental influence is certainly
powerful, but may not survive the teenage years. In other cases
whole dynasties of workers in a particular field may be bred, like
those generations of farmers, and the famous political, medical and
legal families.

On the other hand, many people take a long time to work out and
decide what they want to do in life. One successful local government manager says that he is still waiting to find out what he will
do when he grows up. He has shown progression in his career and
has wide interests, but has only a fuzzy idea of his real aim. That is
no bad thing, and it is a process which will not be hurried in any
case, but at least he is developing contacts and taking on new

challenges which introduce him to new people and situations from which he is constantly learning. In his contacts vertically within his field of work he is meeting, dealing with and impressing the senior people who may well conduct the interviews for his next job. Laterally he meets all kinds of people in other areas of work, which teaches him about opportunities which previously he knew nothing of. What he is doing by accident or design is widening his field of experience. Not knowing which direction to move in, like a mountaineer stuck in fog he stays put until he learns something about the opportunities available. That knowledge tells him which ways to avoid and, by elimination, which directions to explore.

That less decisive approach to career development may invite scorn from those who believe that they know where they are going and how to get there. They are very fortunate people, for the process of self-development is greatly simplified for them. All they have to do is to run along their tramlines far and fast enough and they will go as far as their abilities will carry them. It will doubtless still be hard work, but their certainty is to be envied. For the rest of us, the process of enriching our knowledge of the options available can start immediately. In any case, there is no guarantee that even the most dedicated of us will not wake up one morning to decide to change our aims. Figure 28 shows one approach to looking systematically at your industry and your skills and knowledge to see where opportunities might lie.

That sort of analysis might lead more or less directly to a definition of where you want to go, but it is unlikely. It is much more probable that, like the mountaineer, you can start by deleting the absolutely unacceptable directions. That has its uses for it narrows the field of search. Deletions should not be made prematurely or on the basis of blind prejudice. One of the happiest and most fulfilled of managers once swore that he would never work in the public sector. He now works for a government organisation which uses the full range of his experience in the way that he likes best, with considerable variety and responsibility. Previously he had thought that everyone in the public sector had monotonous jobs and spent their time dodging accountability. That illustrates a point about Figure 28.

The industry in which a person works is made up of all sorts of organisations. They present a rich variety of opportunities to put to work in a different way any experience gained elsewhere in the industry. The skills which the individual has or can acquire add a further dimension. All organisations carry out the functions shown

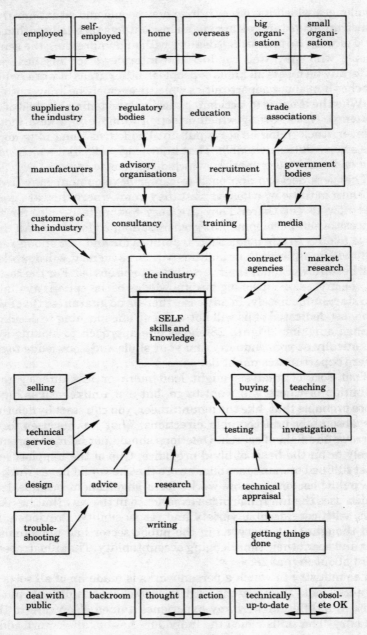

Figure 28 *Areas for career development*

to a lesser or greater extent. The point of this figure is not to offer a fully formed, universally applicable model (for it is not), but to start the first-time manager off on the process of depicting his own situation.

The boxes contain generalised labels which are capable of much sub-division. Indeed they need to be sub-divided to become truly useful; otherwise the happy manager mentioned above would never have come across his odd little patch in the public sector. An exercise like this is not completed in five minutes. Your own plan of the industry and your experience are just the starting points. Each week you could give yourself the job of finding out what options exist within each of the boxes represented, and whether the attitudes and values expressed by those in positions of responsibility coincide with your own. Most organisations publish copious information about their work, and their PR and publicity people will gladly supply as much as you want. The organisations' names and addresses can be found in the directories which are kept in every public library.

The promotable manager

Whether or not you are clear about your future, there remains the present job to be done. The first and minimum task is to hold on to that job: only if you survive in it can you contemplate a brighter future in the present organisation. Moreover, the best way of getting noticed is to do your job well. Doing it well is only a start; you also have to be seen to be doing so. It is dangerous to go too far down the track of self-advertisement, but it is also foolish to conceal the range of good work that you are doing. Remember the words of one cynic, who said that your sole job is to please your boss. Not all bosses are pleased by spaniel-like adoration. Those worth working for know that their own performance depends on the people beneath them, and they look for workmanlike performance without fuss. If you can add an unusual and welcome spark as well, to either your own work or that of the group as a whole – or best of all to both – you will be noticed.

The main characteristic of the promotable person is that he is on top of his job. In that way he demonstrates that he has not reached the summit of what he is capable of, and it is an obvious move to give him a greater challenge.

The way you get noticed is important. Any fool can pass simultaneously into the organisation's folklore as well as unemployment by misbehaving. Wiser people take on the unpopular jobs, provided they can see a way of doing them well. Caution is in order, for most of those jobs are unpopular for a reason, usually that nobody has yet been able to get more out of them than they have to put in. A sober assessment of what can realistically be achieved comes first, and the job is undertaken only if doing it will buy some glory. Then again, letting it be known that you are aware of the drawbacks and still volunteering can earn points for saving everyone else the misery. If it really cannot be done on the resources allocated, offer to take it on but on condition that you are given the tools to do it properly. Then you will be known as the person who pulled off the impossible, and did that dreadful task well.

Another way of demonstrating promotability is to show that you think more widely about the organisation's future than your present job requires you to. Be careful not to look cocky, but if some new technique or idea ought to be applied try it out on your boss. At least you will show that you have a wider field of vision than is normal at your level, and at best you will spark off the organisation's next big breakthrough.

In working with other members of the team, the first-time manager will see their strengths and weaknesses. Some will be good creatively but hopeless as administrators perhaps, others will have sound ideas but be poor at communicating them, and so on. One manager who has understood his colleagues well has a particularly devastating technique in meetings. Many of his colleagues are noisy, creative and talkative. While they all have their say and argue he says nothing. Just as everyone begins to realise that the discussion is getting nowhere he steps in with an incisive analysis of the ideas put forward and follows it with a proposal for action, which is all the more effective for being spoken quietly and slowly. His conclusions are almost always accepted because of the thoroughness with which he thinks his position through, and he has gained a reputation as a deep and thoughtful person. He is clearly a potential chairman of meetings rather than just a participant. His next promotion will be hailed by colleagues as well deserved.

The fastidious person may dislike the idea of pressing for personal advancement. In the culture of some countries it is held to be a perfectly reasonable activity, and in others, particularly northern Europe, it is thought distasteful. If it is done obviously it attracts nothing but derision, and a loss of the credibility so essential to promotion. None of the courses of action advocated is against the interests of the employing organisation and all will have the effect of developing them. Most people who reach positions of great responsibility do so not by politicking but by solid achievement, and having gained the job their grip on it is that much more secure. Most senior managers would be delighted if their first-time managers adopted the approaches suggested in this book. Their lives would be so much easier and their goals would stand a better chance of accomplishment.

Teamwork

The membership of teams has already been touched on. It is an inescapable fact that anyone in a management position is automatically a member of a number of teams. Some of them are semi-permanent in nature and others are set up to deal with a transient situation. Some come about as part of the job and others can be volunteered for. A first-time manager in the transport department, for instance, may automatically be a member of a team which reviews the monthly performance of the distribution function. In his day-to-day operations he is part of the team of drivers, mechanics and clerks. In the former he may be a junior member, in the latter the leader. In turn, he is a subordinate member of the distribution department team. In addition he may be a member of a temporary working party looking at the implications of a major customer's requirement for delivery to 300 shops instead of five regional warehouses. On that team he will work alongside an accountant, a marketing man and a senior salesman. Here his role is different. He is both an expert in the field of transport and a representative of the distribution department. He may also devote one lunch-hour a week to the committee of the sports and social club, where he rubs shoulders informally with people from all levels of the organisation.

Thus the function we undertake and our place in the pecking order vary from team to team across the whole repertoire of teams to which we belong. An official meeting of one team may be followed by that of another. The first-time manager needs a number of skills and a degree of adaptability to handle those transitions successfully. In one meeting he keeps very quiet since the real discussion is taking place at a level well above his own. The reason for attendance is partly a ceremony denoting adulthood, partly to keep the boss in line on any detailed points which may need answering. In that particular role the first-time manager is a very lowly figure. Twenty minutes later he may find himself running a meeting of his section's supervisors. There his style is dramatically different. The team looks to him for a lead; he tries to bring out the contribution which each member undoubtedly has in him to make; he tries gently to induce the noisy ones to allow the quieter members a say. Instead of having all the good ideas himself he tries to get his people to have them, and rewards them when they do. From experience he knows that the practical people who actually have to do the work can straight away see the flaws in any idea for changing the way that they work. They do not always think the problem through analytically, but when they have visualised the way the change would operate they can spot the problem. Knowing this, the manager creates a step-by-step description of what the changes are meant to achieve and how they would work. He encourages interruptions for clarification. He will have planned in advance the way that the meeting will run, starting by defining his objectives for it. The objectives are the sole reason for holding the meeting, after all. Those who have attended the most appallingly chaired meetings which served no useful purpose have determined never to be responsible for such fiascos themselves. They start by deciding what it is for and work from there, constantly referring back to the objective to see if it is being approached by what has been done. New and additional objectives can emerge as the meeting goes on, of course, but the proceedings should repeatedly be examined for signs of progress relative to objectives.

Throughout the discussion of issues involving other people there was repeated reference to the skills involved. Many people think that these are innate: if accidents of birth and upbringing have not conferred them they are beyond a person's grasp. That is a fallacy. It certainly does no harm to get a flying start from nature, but the skills can be learned. The prize for those who take the trouble is great. If the manager's achievement is only the sum of the achievements of the people under him, the better he is at getting them to understand what is necessary and what they could achieve if they really tried, and then infusing them with the will to do it, the better their and his performances will be. Some would say that the art of persuading people to perform to their true potential is the greatest contribution that a human being can make to the sense of achievement and fulfilment of his fellows.

Contacts and career development

The alert first-time manager will not only hone his own skills but will also keep in touch with his environment. He will study and strive to comprehend the shifts in influence within his own organisation; he will seek to understand the constantly changing patterns in the environment which surrounds it and its industry.

To do this he keeps track of the jobs advertised in the industry, as well as watching what happens to people within the organisation, and following their career moves. His attention is not confined to his own organisation and its immediate competitors. He looks upstream to its suppliers and downstream to its customers. He involves himself in industry and professional organisations and makes sure that his significant moves are reported in the trade media. When he joins these organisations he does not content himself with being a foot-soldier, but takes on jobs that need to be done, stands for election and serves on committees. By doing this he contributes to an organisation's fame and reputation, as well as putting a shine on his curriculum vitae. That view is not totally selfless, but there is no rule that says good work should be unrewarded.

As time goes on he may contact a couple of headhunters who specialise in his field of interest, and ring them every six months to keep them up to date with developments in his career. People who do this are often the first to hear of the more interesting jobs which come up.

Inevitably as his career progresses he will meet more and more people with whom he has something in common, even if it is only a shared interest in a profession or an industry. If he sees a chance to help one of them he should take it. It may be with an introduction to a contact, or a reference for a job, or a nomination for a place on a committee, or in some more substantial way. Generosity is a strange commodity: the more of it that is used, the more comes into being. If this sounds like a version of a banality to do with spreading a little happiness, so be it: it does seem to work. Most people harbour generous impulses but need somebody to set them an example. Those who do so create a greater supply of kindness, with a knock-on effect which reverberates and spreads.

Once a congenial contact has been made it should be kept up. The careers of other people are a fascinating study which is highly educational. There is always the possibility that a contact can lead to career advancement, and in any case people who understand your field can be valued advisers in how you could pursue your own ambitions.

Study and training

The first-time manager gives himself a head start in self-development if he refuses to learn from experience alone. His surroundings are packed with opportunities to learn from the mistakes and insights of other people. Libraries run by local authorities, colleges, and professional institutes are full of reading on general and specific aspects of management. Most of them are grouped under Dewey classification number 658 on the bookshelves. The authors most likely to entertain and educate the first-time manager throughout his career are (in my opinion) Peter Drucker, Edward de Bono and Robert Townsend. Drucker is a genius at distilling the essence of the task of a manager, and putting it across in simple language. De Bono is best known for his work on lateral thinking, a powerful and fascinating subject. Townsend is a distinguished manager who has written a book, *Up the Organisation*, subsequently developed into *Further Up the Organisation*, full of serious insights put across hilariously. Those in large organisations, especially in the public sector, will also learn from and relish the books in the *Yes, Minister* series by Lynn and Jay. There are plenty of books around which are written in entirely serious or even impenetrable prose which the first-time manager can find for himself; these serious books which employ lighter language and are more comprehensible are highlighted for a special reason. It is to show that the study of management actually can be fun.

In addition to books, there is the management, professional and industry press to keep up with as well as the quality daily and Sunday newspapers. Those with access to a professional library may also be lucky enough to get hold of academic papers and reports of conference proceedings. The load of reading that this could impose does dictate a certain discipline. It requires a resolution not to read everything. The list of contents of every medium will show which items are relevant enough to warrant dipping into. General reading is skimmed, with stops only at points of definite interest. A rapid reading course, useful for every manager, can help still further.

Many organisations take a positive view of training and are pleased to send staff on courses and seminars and to conferences. Every opportunity of that sort which can be fitted in should be taken. Making the time to do it may not be easy, but the fresh air which it can inject into a manager's thinking is worth it. Moreover, it is another venue for making those useful contacts. Information gained from such sources should not be kept secret, but a brief report should be written and circulated to boss and colleagues. If any of them picks up a point of particular interest, they can interrogate the writer in greater depth.

The same applies to visiting trade exhibitions. They are focal points for what is going on in an industry and must not be missed. A day at one is no beano, but a working day like any other. It is planned and executed in just the same way. And the results obtained are shared with colleagues.

An obvious aspect of the theme of self-education is formal study. The qualifications and skills which it will yield are important, but are far from being the sole reason for undertaking it. All the contacts made with staff and students should be explored to the full, so that personality and experience are broadened. Tutors on courses, whether they are full- or part-time lecturers, often have behind them careers of some eminence. They are frequently engaged currently on projects from which their students can learn a great deal. Many of them take a real interest in their students' future careers and are able and willing to help in its advancement. One manager who was made redundant rang his former tutor for advice, and was offered a temporary lecturing job on the spot: someone had fallen ill and he rang at exactly the right time. He did so well that he was later taken on to the permanent staff, which has opened up a fascinating new career for him. As the first-time manager progresses he can take on some part-time teaching to evening classes to see how it feels. Many managers find it interesting work, and say that the need to re-think how they do their jobs and why, so that they can explain better to the students, is valuable in re-establishing in their own minds how their work should be approached.

Study helps people to develop, not least because it implants habits of thought which help the manager to think more widely and deeply for himself. Over the course of a decade the investment of time is hardly noticed, but it results in the manager becoming quite an expert in his field. He will have seen what works and what does not, will have tested out a few of his own ideas, and have identified who are the real contributors to the field and who are the woolly-minded ones. In any person with a normal ration of assertiveness these conditions bring about a sense of irritation that the world is not run as well as it might be (it never is). That can be closely followed by an urge to put things right by telling the world where it is going wrong. It may start from annoyance at the views expressed in an article in a magazine. A letter or telephone call to the editor could result in an invitation to write an article which proposes a different point of view, and the manager is launched into a secondary career as a writer on his field. Many a manager has done that, and then been approached by publishers who invite him to expand the article into a book. Alternatively, the manager who believes he has a book in him can write to publishers speculatively: there are even books which tell him how to do it for best results. There are plenty of opportunities for improving writing skills. Every organisation's newsletter and industry magazine is avid for articles from people who know their subject, have a clear point of view and can put it across well. Contacts with publishers can lead to requests to review books, and this sort of writing can be noticed so that invitations arrive to deliver papers to conferences. Suddenly that manager finds himself acknowledged as an expert in his field. This status does his prospects no harm, and the whole process involved adds interest to his life.

Active mind in a healthy body

Every manager experiences pressures to become a seven-day week worker who cuts out everything from his life to accommodate his job. Those pressures must be resisted. If they are not, friends will be driven off and eventually even the most understanding family will become alienated. That will cause pain to others as well as to the manager himself, and when adversity strikes, as it will, there will be nobody left to help him through. However tough and self-reliant he may be, there will be times when he needs the solace that only family and friends can provide. If they are to be there when he needs them, he had better be around when they need him.

Moreover, the dispassionate and objective view that can be provided by people who care for him, but who are not themselves directly involved in his work, is a great antidote to the distorted perspective and self-absorption that can arise from total single-mindedness. Thus they help to keep the mind healthy, to keep things in proportion and, above all, to guard against self-importance and pomposity.

Stress is better dealt with by family understanding than by

resort to the various instruments of oblivion like drink, drugs and a surfeit of pleasure. As well as completely failing to improve the situation, indulgence can actually worsen the individual's ability to deal with it. In particular managers should watch themselves for any tendency to reach too often for the most easily available drug, alcohol. Its addictive power is slow to build but devastating once established.

Eating, drinking and the other things that give us legitimate pleasure can all be undertaken, but in moderation. Likewise, a moderate amount of exercise is helpful, though that, too, can be carried to excess. The right amount helps to create a sense of well-being and definitely wards off disease, improves the ability to deal with stress, and generally helps the manager to work better.

The final issue to be raised in this book may be many years away for a number of readers. It concerns the sad fact that in middle life many people feel a dreadful sense of disillusion, wondering what on earth is the point of existence. Even though the time when that problem normally strikes may be far off for many first-time managers, now is the time when they should start to inoculate themselves against it. Keeping fresh mentally, keeping interested in their organisation, their industry and their career, being physically fit, are a good start. Maintaining a healthy social life and being interested in family and friends are important too.

If his career or the organisation are making him miserable, the first-time manager should make a rational calculation of the likelihood of things changing for the better and, if things seem likely to stay the same or get worse for the foreseeable future, he should prepare to move. There should be no delay; immediately that process is begun there will be a lifting of the spirits from the sense that a solution may be possible. There is no excuse for staying put, wasting precious time and cursing fate. The energy consumed is put to far better use in planning an escape. Other people have survived far worse than a sense of futility in their work and come up smiling. They are the sort of personalities who realise that opportunities are there, but only for those who look for them and have prepared themselves to exploit them. A positive attitude to life does not bring a successful outcome every time; negativity almost guarantees failure at every attempt.

Further Reading from Kogan Page

The Business Fact Finder, ed Hano Johannsen, 1987
Don't Do. Delegate! The Secret Power of Successful Managers, James M Jenks and John M Kelly, 1986
Effective Interviewing, John Fletcher, 1988
Essential Management Checklists, Jeffrey P Davidson, 1987
A Handbook of Management Techniques, Michael Armstrong, 1986
How to Be an Even Better Manager, Michael Armstrong, 1988
How to Make Meetings Work, Malcolm Peel, 1988
Make Every Minute Count: How to Manage Your Time Effectively, Marion E Haynes, 1988
Never Take No for an Answer, Samfrits Le Poole, 1987
The Practice of Successful Business Management, Kenneth Winckles, 1986
Profits from Improved Productivity, Fiona Halse and John Humphrey, 1988
Readymade Business Letters, Jim Dening, 1986
So You Think Your Business Needs a Computer, Khalid Aziz, 1986
Winning Strategies for Managing People: A Task Directed Guide, Robert Irwin and Rita Wolenik, 1986

Index